YO-DXD-004

Liberación Nacional in Costa Rica

The Development of a Political Party in a Transitional Society

Burt H. English

University of Florida Press
Gainesville - 1971

320.97286
E

Latin American Monographs — Second Series

Committee on Publications

W. W. McPherson, *Chairman*
Graduate Research Professor
of Agricultural Economics

R. W. Bradbury
Professor of Economics

Raymond E. Crist
Graduate Research Professor
of Geography

Lyle N. McAlister
Professor of History

T. Lynn Smith
Graduate Research Professor
of Sociology

Felicity Trueblood
Assistant Professor
of Comprehensive English

A University of Florida Press Publication

SPONSORED BY THE
CENTER FOR LATIN AMERICAN STUDIES

Series design by Stanley D. Harris

COPYRIGHT © 1971 BY THE STATE OF FLORIDA
BOARD OF TRUSTEES OF THE INTERNAL
IMPROVEMENT TRUST FUND

*Library of Congress
Catalog Card No. 73-107880
ISBN 0-8130-0296-6*

PRINTED IN FLORIDA, U.S.A.

2/10/72   B$T 7.50 (6.75)

Latin American Monographs

Second Series

Liberación Nacional
in Costa Rica

8

Center for Latin American Studies
University of Florida

To Harry Kantor
Teacher, Colleague, Friend

Contents

Tables

Introduction

IT IS ALMOST impossible to think of United States, British, or Soviet politics without thinking of Republicans, Democrats, Laborites, Conservatives, Communists, and so forth. The type of men that govern, the policies they implement, and the methods they employ are all directly related to the nature of partisan affiliations and loyalties. Recent studies have shown that other factors being equal, parties are the greatest explainer of political behavior, whether that behavior be casting a ballot, voting in a legislative assembly, or appointing political elites to administrative positions.

Yet, modern parties are relatively recent phenomena. Few realize that the organizations which seem so important today were unknown in all but a handful of nations just four or five generations ago. Although groups of notables bearing different titles and descriptions fulfilled some of the functions now associated with the modern party, the large, extended, highly structured organizations encouraging mass support and participation are creatures of the nineteenth and twentieth centuries.

This study attempts to analyze the development of the first large permanent party in a small transitional society that is rapidly undergoing a change in political life. A generation ago

Costa Rica was properly considered a sleepy, rural banana republic, out of the mainstream of world events. Today it is becoming increasingly pluralistic, cosmopolitan, city-oriented, commercial — in a word, modern. The transition has necessitated greater sophistication in all fields of endeavor. One of the best examples of such sophistication is the emergence of complex political institutions, the National Liberation Party (PLN) among them. It is hoped that information presented about one party in one nation may be expanded to increase overall understanding of political structures in the less modern parts of the world.

The author maintains most of the normal biases of the social researcher in the West. He believes representative democracy is preferable to authoritarian rule, that ballots are preferable to bullets, and that violent social revolutions are seldom the best solutions to problems and injustices. Furthermore, modern political parties are deemed absolutely necessary in the pluralistic society. Regarding the Costa Rican National Liberation Party, the author is neither liberacionista nor antiliberacionista. The PLN was chosen as an object of study not for favoritism or preference, but because it offers one of the best opportunities to study the phenomenon of party in Central America. If viewed as a continuous organization since the early 1940's, the PLN is undoubtedly the oldest, best organized, most viable modern party on the isthmus. Only the Guatemalan Revolutionary Party and the Salvadorean Renovating Action Party offer serious competition to that claim. At the same time, I believe one cannot undertake a two-year study without becoming a bit fond of the subject. Friendship ties that develop make it difficult to remain totally objective. If the PLN is presented in too favorable a light at times, the reader is invited to interpolate as he desires.

Many persons have given their time and effort to make this study possible, and their help is deeply appreciated. Sharon, the author's wife, did much of the proofreading and all of the typing. Professor Harry Kantor, now of Marquette University, read early drafts and made numerous helpful suggestions throughout the text. The criticisms of the late Professor Charles Farris of the University of Florida were valuable, especially those concerning use of quantitative data in chapters 4, 5, and 6. Professor Lyle McAlister, also of the University of Florida, offered interpretive suggestions pertaining to the historical material in chapters 2 and 3 as well as aiding the research financially in his former capacity as director of the Center for Latin American Studies of the University of Florida. Professor Hugh Popenoe provided the grant which made the study possible through the Caribbean Area Research Program of the University of Florida. An additional research grant from the Ford Foundation administered through the University of Kansas in the summer of 1967 made possible the final preparation of the text. Additional notes of appreciation must go to the many people of the libraries and computing centers of the Universities of Florida and Kansas.

National Liberation Party leaders and other Costa Ricans provided much of the subjective material which led to a better understanding of their country's politics. Particularly helpful were Rodrigo Carazo, president of the 1966 Legislative Assembly; Carlos José Gutierrez, dean of the Faculty of Law of the University of Costa Rica and PLN deputy; Manuel Carballo, secretary general of the Juventud Liberacionista; Salvador Jimenez, director of the Library of the Legislative Assembly; and Milton Clarke, a political scientist at the University of Costa Rica. In addition, Manuel Antonio Quesada made available the large portion of the Archives of the Center for the Study of National Problems, Acción Demócrata, and the Social Democratic Party, which he has guarded throughout the years.

1. Transitional Nature of Contemporary Costa Rican Society

T
HE POLITICAL PARTY is one of the most essential secondary organizations in the modern world. Yet, the actual processes by which viable parties are founded or the societal conditions surrounding their foundation are not fully understood. Therefore, this study was undertaken to trace the development of one political party in a transitional society and ultimately to isolate the most important factors contributing to the successful establishment of such organizations in similar societies. During the postwar generation the National Liberation Party (PLN) developed a record of institutionalization, structuralization, and longevity relatively unique among Latin American parties, a record surpassed only by Mexico's Institutional Revolutionary Party, Venezuela's Democratic Action, Peru's Aprista Party, and a few others. It became an accepted and seemingly perpetual subsystem of the national polity, and has been recognized as something of an innovation by a host of international scholars. As such, it offers an exceptional opportunity to contemporarily analyze the dynamics of political formation and growth in a less-than-modern setting.

Unfortunately, most scholars considering the establishment of political parties have focused their attention on North America and Europe,[1] and even those who have undertaken the study of developing areas in recent years have based their reasoning on the new nations of Africa, Asia, and the Middle East.[2] Consequently, conceptual models, most of which purport to be universal, do not take fully into account the historical experiences in many nations of Latin America. When Latin America is considered at all, the parties in the nations that best fit the model are usually considered, and then only briefly. Typically, parties replace such traditional structures as colonial administrations, closed aristocracies, or military governments; they then seek to integrate, nationalize, and so forth. Yet, even a cursory review of history will illustrate that most republics south of the Rio Grande do not conform to the "typical" pattern. Not counting brief periods of foreign intervention, no Latin American country except Cuba has been under colonial administration for well over a century. Less than half (Peru, Ecuador, El Salvador, Nicaragua, Bolivia, Colombia, Brazil, Chile, and the Dominican Republic before Trujillo) have maintained genuine aristocracies,[3] and only Venezuela, Paraguay, the Dominican Republic, and Haiti have maintained military governments generation after generation. The military[4] was almost always politically active and sometimes assumed direct control, although extended military rule was not the norm. In contrast, much of Latin America was often governed during the traditional period by upper-middle-class members of prominent, influential, or principal families who usually had at heart the best interests of

1. See, for example, Maurice Duverger, *Political Parties: Their Organization and Activity in the Modern State*; and Sigmund Neumann, ed., *Modern Political Parties*.

2. See recent publications of David Apter, Lucian Pye, Gabriel Almond, and Sidney Verba.

3. It is the author's contention that catchalls such as aristocracy and oligarchy are so often used incorrectly with reference to Latin America that great distortion has arisen. All too frequently one hears statements such as "so and so is supported by the oligarchy" or "the wealthy class, allied with the military, did such and such." Except for the countries mentioned above, it seems more meaningful to consider "principal" or "important" families and forget the monolithic inferences of the former terms. The role of such families in traditional Costa Rican politics is considered later in this chapter.

4. It would probably be more accurate to refer to "military elements" during the traditional era, because professional armies were not established in most Latin American countries until the 1900–1935 period. Previously, partisan or private bands had served as military units.

their nations. These rulers might often have been inept or otherwise unqualified to fulfill their goals, but the types of governments they administered were certainly much different from those presented as "traditional" in most conceptual models.

Likewise, many of the governing notables during the traditional period undertook programs of integration and nationalization. Again, the total effectiveness of their programs might be questioned, but the model of a small and compact colonial or native elite running things to their own advantage and to the detriment of the general populace is not accurate. The author contends that in about half the countries of Latin America between 1830 and 1945 the number of rulers who tried to emulate Sarmiento and Juarez was larger than the number that imitated Rosas and Santa Anna.

Of the various approaches to the study of parties in developing areas, that suggested by LaPalombara and Weiner seems to be most useful and will be employed in this study.[5] Central to their notion of party is the aspect of modernness for which they have established four essential characteristics — characteristics which all "modern" parties presumably possess, but which other political groups such as cliques, clubs, and groups of notables do not, even though they might operate under the party label. First, the party must be continuous; it must possess an organizational sophistication great enough to enable it to carry on after any particular leaders or group of leaders have departed the political scene. Second, it must be permanently organized at local levels, and the leaders of the local units must interact and communicate on a regular basis with national leaders. Third, both local and national leaders must make a determined effort to control the decision-making apparatus of the nation and not just seek to influence decision-makers who are not affiliated with the partisan organization. Fourth, the modern party must seek popular support in some manner. In addition, a variation of the modern party, the "modernizing" party with a definite mission to transform the society, will possess a fifth characteristic, an elaborate and reasonably well-defined ideology.

This study analyzes the National Liberation Party in light of these five factors. It attempts, through the use of archival, electoral, and interview data, to describe the organization's origins,

5. Joseph LaPalombara and Myron Weiner, "The Origin and Development of Political Parties," in *Political Parties and Political Development.*

bases of support, local and national leadership cadres, and ideology with the goal of determining how modern parties are established in transitional societies. Chapters 2, 3, and 4 consider the first criterion, that modern parties must be continuous, by tracing the historical development of the PLN. Chapter 5 analyzes the party with respect to the second criterion, that permanent local units must exist, and chapter 6 deals with both the third and fourth criteria. The latter two, that the modern party must make a determined effort to gain political power and that it must seek popular support, are considered together for the obvious reason that in a democratic society both are directly tied to elections. Fifth, chapters 7 and 8 consider party ideology as an aspect of the modernizing mission of a modern party. Finally, the PLN is considered against LaPalombara and Weiner's three theories of party development in chapter 9, and final conclusions are presented at that point. It is hypothesized that the PLN does possess all five essential characteristics and has become one of the first modern parties in Costa Rica and the rest of Central America. However, before examining the conditions which brought about its establishment, it will first be necessary to consider the key aspects of the traditional Costa Rican political system and the way in which the system has been undergoing rapid transition in recent decades.

The Nature of the Traditional Costa Rican Political System

Costa Rica, a very small country with an area of 19,650 square miles, began its independent political existence with less than 70,000 persons, most of whom lived from subsistence agriculture on an isolated mountainous plateau. Until the outbreak of World War II, politics were very simple, and executive power was transferred in a relatively peaceful (although not very democratic) method from incumbent to selected inheritor. As a general rule, each outgoing president "willed" the political and economic support that had kept him in office to a successor who then used that support to win a controlled or influenced election.[6] Although periods of turmoil were not unknown,[7] the

6. After 1891 a few reasonably honest elections were held, but the overall tradition remained intact. An indirect voting system was employed as late as 1913.

7. During the 146 years of independence from 1824 to 1970, one president was executed, eight more were illegally deposed, and five resigned their office. Of the nineteen chiefs of state in power during the nineteenth century, ten were

nation was far more stable than its neighbors.[8] There has never been a Juan Manuel Rosas, a Rafael Trujillo, or a Juan Vicente Gomez in Costa Rica. In such a simple, stable, and peaceful society, complex organizations were not needed, and although temporary political groups appeared from time to time, no permanent structure ever existed.

According to the Census of 1844, only 73,906 persons populated the area of the Meseta Central (including Cartago), which was for all practical purposes the entire range of the national political system of the day.[9] Because travel outside the Meseta was so difficult, the 5,193 inhabitants of Guanacaste and the 883 of Puntarenas each formed small, self-contained, autonomous societies that were virtually out of the pale of national political influence. Within the Meseta travel was easy, distances between towns were short, and the small population made it possible for nearly every politically active person to be acquainted, either directly or through family and friendship ties, with nearly every other. Modern political parties were simply not needed in the days when an individual could get things done by conferring with a relative, a parish priest, a *gamonal* (local political leader), or other notable of easy access. True, there were two mainstreams of ideology, the liberal and conservative, around which certain families and other groups clustered, but any kind of permanent structure was almost totally lacking.[10]

Another reason why modern parties were unnecessary involved not only the question of access to political channels, but

---

either deposed or obtained their office illegally. Until very recently, elections were openly fraudulent and, if held at all, were held to impress foreigners. The author witnessed a series of street fights, armed attacks, and explosions in conjunction with the 1966 presidential campaign, in which four persons were seriously wounded. For days after the election, rumors of revolt and revolution filled the capital. Charges and countercharges of fraud and illegal electoral practices were quite prevalent.

8. The thirty-three presidents of the 1824–1967 period served an average term of 4.33 years. This is even more impressive when it is kept in mind that only five presidents served 8 years or longer.

9. Dirección General de Estadística y Censos, *1864 Censo de Población*, p. 3. The 1864 census report contains the totals of the 1844 census.

10. A similar situation apparently existed in North America during the colonial period and early days of nationhood. William Nisbet Chambers states that: "Despite the persistence of loosely applied labels like Whig and Tory, which actually denoted general persuasions rather than distinct political formation, there were no parties in the proper or modern sense." See Chambers, *Political Parties in a New Nation: The American Experience, 1776–1809*, p. 4.

overall governmental activity as well. The political and economic culture of the period emphasized individual responsibility, a laissez faire doctrine of state intervention, and an overall attitude of negative government. Desired or expected governmental actions were few in number—protection from foreign invasion, maintenance of order, and the provision of a few essential services, such as the construction of roads, bridges, and so forth.

This absence of political demands, both in terms of complexity and number, caused electoral campaigns to be little more than popularity contests involving the relative merits of certain candidates over others, with the "officially approved" candidate having an obvious advantage.[11] Aside from the religious controversy which flared up briefly in the 1880's and 1890's, crucial issues centered around honesty, administrative talent, appearances, and family background. Ideological questions were little considered and given scant attention. A Costa Rican student of his nation's social problems has adequately described the personalist pattern of politics during the nineteenth and early twentieth centuries:

> Political parties with definite ideas do not exist in Costa Rica. Every four years, in the year before the presidential term expires, as many groups organize themselves for the electoral campaign which is about to begin, as there are candidates. The political parties organize themselves around a man of merit and sufficient prestige to attract public attention. The distinction between the parties is reduced to adding the syllables *ista* to the name of the candidate, and with this and an insignia of one or more colors, the party is ready to enter fully into an ardent struggle utilizing the press, personal propaganda, speeches, parades, and insults of the opposing candidates.... The struggle ended, the waters regain their normal level, the insults are forgotten, and enthusiasm dies down, and life returns to its normal condition of complete tranquility to repeat itself with the same procedure four years later with another name and its indispensable *ista*.[12]

11. Although an indirect system of voting was employed during most of the period under consideration, presidential electors were generally considered to be supporters of one candidate or another.

12. Alberto Quijano Quesada, *Costa Rica ayer y hoy*, p. 33, cited by Harry Kantor, *The Costa Rican Election of 1953: A Case Study*, p. 34. Translation is Kantor's.

Although modern political parties did not exist, it would be a mistake to imply that the functions generally associated with parties—recruitment, politicization, interest aggregation and articulation, nomination—went unfulfilled. In traditional Costa Rica these patterns were carried on by ostensibly nonpolitical structures such as the family, the Roman Catholic Church, the Masonic Lodge, and to a lesser extent the army. Of the three, families were by far the most important. The Biesanzes wrote: "Each town has a group of families known as the *familias principales*, whose status has been secure for several generations. These are so interrelated that it is asserted that all presidents— except three whose ancestors came from other countries—are related. Some of the principal families claim noble Spanish ancestry...."[13] Political actors were recruited from among those families, and political elites were nominated by them. Administrative positions were given to relatives of decision-makers, and sons of powerful families were assured political careers for the asking.[14]

The Roman Catholic Church and the Masonic Lodge also fulfilled the behavior patterns of political parties, especially during the twenty-year period of religious conflict. Freemasonry, although not as politically aggressive as in Mexico and Guatemala, had long opposed certain Church prerogatives, especially those dealing with education. In the final decades of the nineteenth century the Masons became the principal proponents of classical liberal ideas, and the hierarchy of the Church, in turn, articulated conservative interests, recruited supporters, and at times even nominated candidates for public offices.[15] The highest

13. John and Mavis Biesanz, *Costa Rican Life*, p. 21.

14. Gonzalo Chacon Trejos amply illustrates the predominance, prestige, and power of the "social" families of the past century in his collection of historical anecdotes, *Tradiciones Costarricenses*.

15. Consider, for example, this account of an attempt to recruit an aged *gamonal* (local leader) during what must have been the election of 1890:

"... Does señor Juan Álvarez live here?" asked the voice [from outside the house].

"Yes, señor. Come in," answered [the *gamonal's* wife].

"May God give you a very good night," said the new arrival, entering the house. "May the Lord make you all saints."

"... Have the goodness to be seated, señor," said [the wife].

"Many thanks, señora, but first I wish to know one thing: this house, is it of God, or of the devil?"

"Of God, señor!" exclaimed the frightened woman.

"Very well, then you are of the Nationalist Party."

peak in the religious struggle was reached from 1890 to 1894 when Archbishop Bernardo A. Thiel organized the politically active clergy and laity into the National Union Party. In an open attempt to gain direct access to national decision-making structures, Thiel instructed the faithful: "It is urgent that Catholics devote themselves to this organization and commit their persons and financial possessions to each other, because simple prayer, whether undertaken at church or at home, will not set things right. Actions and financial contributions are needed along with other duties."[16] Half a century later Archbishop Sanabria recognized the political behavior of the Church at that time, "each priest was converted into a political propagandist and every parish and each important neighborhood into a political club."[17]

Although less important in traditional Costa Rican society than in that of its neighbors, the army did, to a certain extent, assume the duties of a political party. Rafael Obregón Loria lists forty instances in Costa Rican history in which the military directly attempted to seize political control.[18] Three military men served as President of the Republic[19] and two more served as designates for brief periods. During the dictatorships of General Tomás Guardia (1870–81) and Federico Tinoco (1917–19) the military directly nominated officers and sympathetic

---

"... A Christian as honorable as [the *gamonal*] cannot be with the Masons, who are going to burn the churches.

[The *gamonal*] felt terrified on hearing this.

"And of what party are you?" the wife mustered courage to ask.

"I? Of the party of our Lord. Now you see my candidate — " and on saying this he drew a crucifix out of his breast pocket, the feet of which he kissed with devotion. The whole family remained awestruck before this act of piety....

The above account is from "La Política," in Ricardo Fernandez Guardia, *Cuentos Ticos* (*Short Stories of Costa Rica*), pp. 154–55. The local *jefe político*, schoolteacher, and others supported the "Progressive Party" (the author's pseudonym for the Progressive Liberal Party) while the Church hierarchy strongly favored the "Nationalist Party" (i.e., the Constitutional Democratic Party). The former was accused of being controlled by the "Godless Masonic Antichrists," while the latter was painted as a club of despotic priests. Although ostensibly fiction, the account is amazingly perceptive in its description of the temporary, shifting, and extremely unstructured "parties" which in reality were controlled by structures of other social systems.

16. Cited by Carlos Monge A., *Historia de Costa Rica*, 5th ed., p. 190.

17. Ibid.

18. *Conflictos militares y políticos de Costa Rica.*

19. General Francisco Morazán, 1842; General Tomás Guardia, 1870–81; and General Próspero Fernandez, 1882–85.

civilians to fill major administrative posts and provided a channel whereby clever and ambitious youths of the middle classes could gain direct access to the political system through a military career. Again, it must be emphasized that the military fulfilled the functions of political parties only intermittently and in a limited fashion. Professor Busey has correctly observed that: "Even where the military have intervened in political affairs and have succeeded in overthrowing Costa Rican governments, they have tended to withdraw and to leave the question of presidential succession to civilian deliberation. This accounts for the seemingly odd fact that more governments have been overthrown than have been replaced by armed force."[20]

The Transitional Nature of Contemporary Costa Rican Society

The Great Depression and World War II upset the traditional system of Costa Rica. Lowered living conditions in the 1930's stimulated some of the more alert young men into accelerated political activity, and new organizations were created, among them the Communist Party and the student discussion clubs that later formed part of the PLN. The newer groups had little impact on national politics until the 1940's, but it was their activities and ideas which began to change the pattern of politics. The contemporary political system, developed in the aftermath of the 1948 War of National Liberation, employs many more complex structures and can be considered more "modern." This is not to suggest that behavioral overlapping no longer occurs, yet a great change has taken place with respect to political differentiation and this change is nowhere more noticeable than with political parties. Elite families find it far more difficult to nominate political decision-makers and family origin means less today.[21] The Church and military are even less concerned with the enumerated political functions. The military, handicapped since 1948 by a device which has changed up to 90 per cent of its officer corps every four years,[22] has not recently had

20. James L. Busey, "The Presidents of Costa Rica," p. 61.

21. The Biesanzes cite the statement of a thirty-year-old woman: "When I was in high school and a girl of the upper class gave a party, she knew exactly whom she should invite and whom she should not, for it was understood that this person 'belonged' and that one did not. Now it is hard to tell; class lines are not sharp." *Costa Rican Life*, pp. 20–21.

22. For information concerning the Costa Rican military, see Wayne L. Worthington, "The Costa Rican Public Security Forces: A Model Armed Force for Emerging Nations?"

the capacity to undertake its former political activities. In contrast to earlier days there are at least four (more or less) permanently organized political parties with some structuralization. Of the four, the PLN was undoubtedly the largest and most complex during the generation under consideration.

It has been implied that societies making the transition from a traditional, agricultural, family-oriented base to a more modern, industrial, pluralistic one will at some time in their development reach a point at which the old political structures no longer suffice. At that point, modern political parties will appear and replace them.[23] "In America," writes Chambers, "party development was caught up in such an unfolding, energizing process. Parties could emerge as political formations which were 'modern' or even 'popular,' because the nation was becoming 'modern' and 'democratic.' At the same time, they could help it on its way."[24] The same theme is emphasized by LaPalombara and Weiner: "Thus one might argue that, just as bureaucracy emerged when public administration could no longer be adequately handled in the prince's household, the political party materialized when the tasks of recruiting political leadership and making public policy could no longer be handled by a small coterie of men unconcerned with public sentiment."[25] This is not to imply that modern parties will automatically and mysteriously burst full-grown upon the political scene simply because the time for them becomes opportune. Hypothesizing such a spontaneous process of generation would not only discredit the work of party founders, but provide an erroneous model, for a party is "a product of human ingenuity and not simply of natural growth. It must be built by the efforts of skilled political craftsmen. . . ."[26]

In conclusion, the National Liberation Party will be analyzed in terms of the five major characteristics of modern political parties outlined by LaPalombara and Weiner. Many approaches

23. This is assuming, of course, that the society is essentially democratic, in that private political interest groups are allowed to operate within the legal framework of the political system. When those groups are frustrated by authority suppression, they will be driven underground and probably emerge as mass revolutionary societies bent on destroying the political system which denies them legitimate functions.

24. Chambers, *Political Parties*, p. 15.

25. LaPalombara and Weiner, *Political Parties*, pp. 3–4.

26. Chambers, *Political Parties*, p. 20.

to the study of parties are possible and indeed beneficial because they tend to bring out shortcomings and inconsistencies in each other. No implication is made that the one used in this study focuses on all important aspects of the party under consideration. It is believed, however, that this approach does point up major questions of concern for the student of politics. Underlying this belief is the assumption that shedding light on the major variables cited will increase knowledge of the processes by which highly structuralized political parties become established in transitional societies, how they function internally, and how they, in turn, affect the total society.

2. The Center for the Study of National Problems and Democratic Action

I T IS IMPOSSIBLE to pinpoint the exact date when a purely traditional society becomes a more modern pluralistic one. Indeed, the process is usually slow and accumulative, involving years if not decades.[1] One innovation creates need for another; one new social group or organization adds but an additional link to an ever increasing chain. Nevertheless, by 1940 the overall Costa Rican society had reached that theoretical point in its development when political parties became imperative. The decade of the 1940's was a period of nearly total political change because the complexity of the society would no longer permit the informal pattern outlined in the previous chapter.

At the beginning of the decade of transition, individuals later to become important organizers and leaders of the National Liberation Party were not involved in politics for the most part. The majority were students, others were young professionals or businessmen. Essentially, the foundation of the party is the history of two groups: the Center for the Study of National Problems and Democratic Action. The development of the PLN and other Costa Rican political parties is illustrated in Figure 1.

1. Even nations experiencing violent social revolution do not change traditional patterns and traditional behavior overnight. In all cases, a relatively long period of time is needed to accomplish significant change.

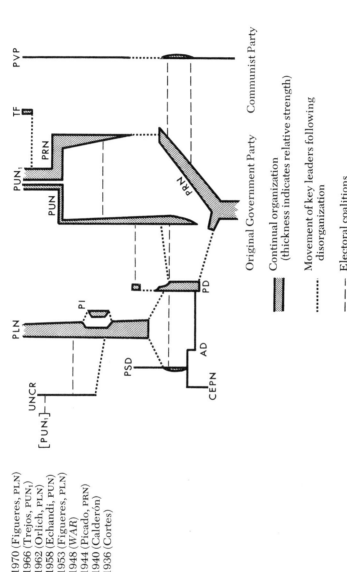

Figure 1. The Costa Rican political party system, 1936–70. Position on the diagram in no way reflects ideology. Indicated on the left are election years, victors, and party. CEPN, Center for the Study of National Problems; AD, Democratic Action; PSD, Social Democratic Party; UNCR, Civic-Revolutionary National Union; PI, Independent Party; PLN, National Liberation Party; PD, Democratic Party; PUN, National Union Party; PUN, National Unification Party; PRN, National Republican Party; TF, Third Front; PVP, Popular Vanguard Party.

1970 (Figueres, PLN)
1966 (Trejos, PUN₁)
1962 (Orlich, PLN)
1958 (Echandi, PUN)
1953 (Figueres, PLN)
1948 (WAR)
1944 (Picado, PRN)
1940 (Calderón)
1936 (Cortes)

PVP

TF

PRN

PUN₁

PUN

PRN

Original Government Party   Communist Party

Continual organization
(thickness indicates relative strength)

Movement of key leaders following
disorganization

Electoral coalitions

PLN

PI

PD

PSD

AD

CEPN

UNCR

[PUN₁]

The Center for the Study of National Problems

The origin of the Center for the Study of National Problems can be traced to the mid-1930's when Carlos Monge Alfaro and Felipe Azofeifa, teachers at the secondary school Liceo de Costa Rica in San José, began meeting on an informal basis with their students to discuss problems of Costa Rican society. Monge, not much older than his pupils, believed a country's youth to be its most important national resource, but like any national resource it must be developed in order to bring benefits.[2] In this respect the two teachers likened youth to a precious although difficult gold mine. Their concept of education involved the formulation of character and sentiment by developing the individual's talents. Above all, youth had to be impressed with a critical attitude concerning every aspect of scholarship. Monge and Azofeifa insisted that their students question even what they themselves might teach. Because they did not feel this type of education could be undertaken without direct contact on a basis of close friendship, they started informal discussion groups dedicated to the pursuit of academic interests. Out of those informal discussions grew the Cultural Association of Law Students in 1939. The new association was primarily centered in the Faculty of Law at the newly established University of Costa Rica, but soon professors and students from other disciplines, particularly agronomy, displayed interest and participated actively. To accommodate the new members, the association changed its name to the Federation of Students and affiliated with student movements in other Central American republics. It should be strongly emphasized that the small federation was not associated with any partisan force in the nation. It limited itself to the discussion of broad economic and political questions, international affairs, and cultural development.

By 1940 it had attracted several dozen members from outside the university. Secondary school teachers, reporters, writers, a few office workers, and others had joined and were becoming increasingly active. To rid itself of the stereotype of a purely university organization, the group again changed its name, this time to the Center for the Study of National Problems. The newly formed Center survived less than a year because of an internal

2. Most of the background material was obtained during an interview with Professor Carlos Monge Alfaro, rector of the University of Costa Rica, January 17, 1966. See also Alberto F. Cañas, *Los 8 años*.

controversy over the 1940 presidential election. The members remained close, however, and shortly after the election met at the home of Roberto Brenes Mesén in order to continue their discussions. At that point a decision was made to reinstitute the Center, and the group began meeting Tuesday evenings in a San José soda shoppe. Later it met in the home of Gonzalo Facio and in 1941 rented a second floor office in a downtown building.

The Center began publishing a monthly journal, *Surco*, in June 1940. In its early years *Surco* was primarily a cultural and literary effort which contained articles relating to Costa Rican history, anthropology, and culture as well as poems, short stories, and book reviews. Although the group's doctrine and ideology will be covered more fully in a subsequent chapter, it should be noted that the themes of democracy and social reform composed a central thesis in articles published by Center members. The social legislation of the Roosevelt administration was usually adopted as a model for the group's program, and members studying or working in the United States often sent articles relating their experiences and concepts of North American democracy.[3] The editor's report for the 1942–43 fiscal year states that the journal published one thousand issues per month and operated on an average monthly budget of $23.20 (U.S.).[4] A list of subscribers for May 1943 shows that 557, or more than half the total monthly readers, resided in the capital.[5]

Besides its journal, the Center made use of two daily Costa Rican newspapers and a radio station after 1942. Otilio Ulate, publisher of the *Diario de Costa Rica*, included a weekly column entitled "Acción del Centro" in his paper; a similar column also appeared in *La Hora*, and in 1943 radio station "Voz de la Democracia" included an hour-long program on Thursday evenings.

3. See, for example, an article by Harvard law student Fernando Fournier, "Los Estados Unidos de F. D. Roosevelt," *Surco*, no. 15 (Aug., 1941), pp. 10–11. Although the Center usually adopted a pro-United States attitude, instances of anti-Americanism can be noted. For example, a 1942 report by the Center's foreign relations study section concludes a review of Nearing and Freeman's *Dollar Diplomacy* with the following phrase: "BECOME A MEMBER OF THE CENTER FOR THE STUDY OF NATIONAL PROBLEMS AND LEARN HOW TO CONTROL THE ENORMOUS NORTH AMERICAN IMPERIALIST ECONOMIC FORCES IN OUR COUNTRY!!!!" Archives of the Center for the Study of National Problems, San José.

4. Archives of the Center for the Study of National Problems, San José. Costa Rican colones were converted to United States dollars at the then current rate of 5.60 to 1.

5. Ibid.

Center members began publishing occasional articles in practically all Costa Rican newspapers and periodicals, and with increased publicity came new members. It should be stated at this point that membership was always very selective and by invitation only; there was never any attempt to turn the Center into a mass youth movement. Treasury records show that in 1940 the group had a total membership of fifty-nine and a monthly income of about $20 (U.S.), most of which accrued from small dues. Similarly, an Executive Committee report for 1941, submitted on February 28, 1942, shows that in the preceding twelve months only twenty-two new initiates had been admitted.[6] The same slow but regular growth rate was maintained thereafter, and at the time of the Center's merger in March 1945, it counted about 200 affiliates.

The Center sought to improve its popular image by offering free cultural courses to the general public. A typical course in political economy was taught weekly by Center members under the general leadership of Rodrigo Facio in the Manuel Aregón Business School. Individual lectures dealt with such widely diverse subjects as production, distribution, socialism, fascism, neo-liberalism, the Mexican Revolution, problems of coffee and banana production, electrification, money and credit, and public finance. It is not known how many persons took advantage of the courses nor how regular attendance remained, but judging from the enthusiasm of correspondence between Center officers the results must have been satisfactory.

Study commissions, each composed of ten to fifteen active members, were sponsored by the Center. Separate commissions were instituted for economic affairs, public finance, education, agriculture, industry, interior government, labor, justice and religion, health, and foreign relations. They were planned in order to closely parallel Costa Rican governmental ministries, and several commissions worked quite closely with their respective official counterparts. Every Center member was put on one or more commissions and graded by his respective chairman according to quality of work and attendance. The *cédulas* (identification booklets) of all members contained spaces for recording such participation and grades received therefrom.

The Center also concentrated much energy on organizing the

6. Ibid.

new University of Costa Rica. In 1941 a special committee which included Gonzalo Facio, Gilbert Laporte, Carlos Monge, and Rodrigo Facio undertook an investigation of the curriculum which eventually led to the creation of a School of Commerce and Economics. At the same time a detailed plan suggesting changes in the curriculum of the School of Liberal Arts was presented to the national Minister of Education for consideration. The Center, however, never limited itself strictly to university problems; it campaigned actively against a 1941 law designed to reduce municipal representation and made the establishment of co-operatives its chief economic goal. Not only producers' and consumers' cooperatives but organizations designed to provide public services for specific areas were strongly encouraged. Of primary interest among the latter type were cooperatives for electrification.[7]

The year between July 1943 and June 1944 marked a watershed for the young organization. The political campaign preceding the 1944 presidential election was by far the most violent in the nation's history to that point, and new and far reaching issues threatened to upset the previously described stability. Popular ex-President Leon Cortes had split from the loosely organized coalition of government employees and important families which had been responsible for electing a series of presidents and sought re-election under the banner of the hastily organized Democratic Party (also called the Cortesista Party). The followers of the incumbent president, Rafael Calderón Guardia, had organized as the National Republican Party (PRN) and supported Teodoro Picado, a close friend of the chief executive. In addition, Calderón had signed a coalition agreement with Manuel Mora, head of the Communist Popular Vanguard Party (PVP), creating the Bloque de la Victoria. The effects of World War II complicated the situation even more; by late 1943 each side accused the other of sedition, treason, or worse. Cortesistas accused the government of harboring strong Communist and totalitarian sympathizers and used the existence of the PRN–PVP coalition as proof, while the followers of Calderón and Mora charged that the opposition was simultaneously dominated by the Axis and the United States. The following paid Communist advertisement published less than a month before

7. See the special issue on cooperatives in *Surco*, no. 31 (Jan., 1943), especially Rodrigo Facio, "Ensayos cooperativos en Costa Rica," pp. 30–33.

the election is noteworthy as an example of the type of campaign literature appearing that year:

WE ACCUSE THE FOLLOWERS OF CORTES OF INTENDING THE CRIME OF TREASON: THE SOVEREIGNTY OF COSTA RICA IS IN DANGER. . . .

The directors of the Cortesista Party, whom we crucify by accusing betrayal of the Fatherland, have no other purpose, no greater hope, nor any more fervent ideal than foreign intervention in Costa Rica. Knowing that legally they will not be able to beat us . . . Cortes and his followers have only one hope, to sell the sovereignty of the Fatherland. . . . Roberto Brenes Mesén [the Center's informal advisor] left for the United States to ask for foreign intervention and to fill the Yankee newspapers with insults against the Costa Rican people. . . . [The opposition] . . . has sent diplomats to [Guatemalan strongman] Jorge Ubico to intervene in Costa Rica and put Leon Cortes in the presidency. Many facts can be demonstrated to give credence that Cortes and his followers are disposed to terminate the liberty of Costa Rica, extinguishing it forever with foreign intervention.[8]

In a similar vein, a Communist newsletter called the Center for the Study of National Problems a "sickness of the petty-bourgeois intellectuals."[9] Although the Center did not formally support Cortes, almost all of its members were openly sympathetic to him as individuals. Articles written by centristas in *La Nación* and the *Diario de Costa Rica* denounced the slander and beatings of Cortesistas by followers of Calderón and Mora.[10] The opposition charged the subsequent election represented fraud and political chicanery at its worst. At this point the Center began changing from a small, closed discussion group to a dynamic participant in Costa Rican politics. Current PLN leaders who were involved in the Center at the time explain their reac-

8. *Diario de Costa Rica* (Jan. 5, 1944), p. 2.
9. "Socialismo y Cultura" (Sept. 21, 1944).
10. Both sides charged that their sympathizers were being beaten and mugged as a result of the campaign. For example, in another paid advertisement, the Communists published the photograph of a bandaged citizen with the following explanation: "This photograph is of don RECAREDO SIBAJA MONTERO, who was treacherously attacked by three cortesistas sent by their leaders . . . for the 'crime' of having expressed his opinion as a citizen against the fratricidal ambition of Leon Cortes." *Diario de Costa Rica* (Jan. 5, 1944), p. 2. Reasonable estimates of the number of deaths directly resulting from the political turmoil run as high as twenty-five.

tions to the events of 1943–44 in terms of shock and abhorrence; they felt something would have to be done to prevent such circumstances from recurring and began discussing the possibility of founding a new political party.

Another opportunity for the Center to enter into active politics came as a result of a vow made by publisher Otilio Ulate to close down the *Diario de Costa Rica* if freedom of the press were not permitted in conjunction with the 1944 election. He kept his vow, and the *Diario* stopped publication on February 8. In a dilemma over financial loss if the paper remained closed or embarrassment for failing to keep his vow, Ulate asked the Center to assume its management,[11] and the *Diario* reappeared on February 18, edited by a committee composed of Oton Acosta, Rodrigo Facio, and Jorge Rossi. The tone of subsequent editorials attests the changed attitude of the Center. Whereas it had always attacked the personalism, favoritism, lack of ideology, and other shortcomings of the Costa Rican political system *as a whole*, it began attacking the Calderón-Picado-Mora administration in particular.[12]

The Center's formal organizational structure was also changed in order to give it a more militant and partylike appearance. It lost its identity as a small discussion group and became increasingly complex. Sections were organized in outlying provinces, and a national directorate began coordinating the work of local sections. A *sección centrista* was defined as "a group, large or small, but compact and determined, of persons of clean private or public life, that organize in a city, a town, or village of any province of the Republic, in order to study respective local problems, to acquire a centrista political conscience, and to develop in general their intellectual capacities, in the benefit

11. Interview with University of Costa Rica Law School Dean Carlos José Gutierrez (Mar. 15, 1966). Dean Gutierrez maintained that the talks with Ulate which led to the Center taking over publication of the *Diario* lasted only several hours.

12. A special election issue of *Surco* studied the Calderón administration in depth and was highly critical of it, see no. 47 (May and June, 1944). Also indicative of the Center's new attitude are Hernán Gonzalez Gutierrez, "El sistema personalist político," *Surco*, no. 36 (June, 1943), pp. 15–17; "Ante el pacto Republicano Nacional-Vanguardia Popular," *Surco*, no. 40 (Oct., 1943), pp. 1–6; and "Teoría y realidad del 'Bloque de la Victoria,'" *Surco*, no. 51 (Dec., 1944 and Jan., 1945), pp. 1–4. Also see centrista editorials in the *Diario de Costa Rica* after February 18, 1944, especially "El 'Centro' llama a la compactación," Feb. 18, 1944, p. 1.

of a great ideological action to work in the future for a National Democratic Renewal."[13] The movement to broaden the geographical base closely corresponded in time to the election of a new directorate headed by Rafael Zúñiga. Heredia became the first locality outside the capital to establish a separate body in March 1943, although that group had functioned informally since July of the previous year. The following month, April 1943, saw the formation of a second section in Cartago and the preliminary negotiations for an Alajuela group. The cities of Puntarenas, Liberia, Santa Cruz, Nicoya, and Turrialba soon followed.

Greater expansion necessitated greater sophistication in the rules regulating internal organization and recruitment. The governing boards of local sections were composed of a president, a secretary, a treasurer, plus two others and were responsible to the Department of Sections of the National Center.[14] In addition, sectional commissions, each with a counterpart in the national organization, specialized in specific areas of endeavor; for example, cooperative commissions sought to encourage the cooperative movement in local areas. Gone were the days when students and others simply affiliated with the Center on a relatively informal basis and referred to their organization as "a group of friends united by our fondness of study. . . ."[15] After 1944 new members had to be formally invited to local sections and show proof of intellectual capacity and character. If approved by the directorate and a majority of the total members of the section, probationary status was granted for a period of several months during which time the sectional president was obligated to send monthly progress reports to the chairman of the Sectional Department. Full-status membership was awarded by the National Center upon successful completion of the probationary period.

The Center changed from a nonpartisan to a partisan organization in two other ways. First, members began referring to each other as centristas, thus fostering a sense of group identification. A motion put before the Center's assembly by a group of members suggested changing the name of the entire organiza-

13. "Información sobre las Secciones del Centro," *Surco*, no. 35 (May, 1943), p. 5.
14. Jorge Rossi served as the first chairman of that department.
15. Centro para el Estudio de Problemas Nacionales, "Quienes somos."

tion to Acción Centrista, thus giving it a much more dynamic appearance. The motion would have kept the name Center for the Study of National Problems to refer only to the central unit in San José.[16] Second, by 1944 the Center had acquired enough stability in its leadership nucleus to allow active political participation. A brief review of that leadership reveals turnover at top levels had been held to a minimum. Its president, Rafael Alberto Zúñiga, had been a former editor of *Surco* and had been influential in shaping its ideology; Secretary Manuel Antonio Quesada played an active role as an organizer in the 1943–45 period; Daniel Oduber had been one of the original centristas, an early director of *Surco*, and a steadfast leader since the late 1930's; Rodrigo Facio remained the Center's undeclared intellectual leader; Roberto Brenes Mesén, a retired Northwestern University professor, continued in his role as informal advisor and lent continuity to the group; Gonzalo Facio, Alberto Cañas, Isaac Azofeifa, Carlos Monge, Jorge Rossi, Oton Acosta, Carlos José Gutierrez, and Fernando Fournier also continued their roles as centrista activists. In short, as a result of the presidential campaign of 1943–44, the Center for the Study of National Problems acted less and less like a student discussion group and more and more like a political movement or a political party.[17]

By mid-1944, the Center had definitely become a leadership cadre for a strong and disciplined party. Why did a small student discussion group evolve into that type of organization? Part of the answer involved the crisis of World War II and the threat of communism. Due to the tradition of strictly personalist politics, parties in Costa Rica were only temporary coalitions designed to further the candidacy of a single individual and offered almost no means of registering protest against an unpopular government; therefore, dissatisfied elements had to establish new vehicles of expression. Perhaps an even more important reason

16. *Actas Oficiales* (May, 1944), Archives of the Center for the Study of National Problems, San José.
17. Of special interest in demonstrating the changing attitude of the group in this respect are Luis F. Morúa, "Hacía la formación de un partido de frente único," *Surco*, no. 37 (July, 1943), pp. 20–22; "El país está maduro para la formación de un partido ideológico democrático," *Surco*, no. 42 (Jan., 1943), pp. 1–3; "Hacía la formación del Partido Político Doctrinario: El Centro es un organización permanente," *Diario de Costa Rica* (Feb. 23, 1944), p. 1; "El país está maduro para vivir en un régimen de Partidos Ideológicos," *Diario de Costa Rica* (Mar. 3, 1944), p. 1; and "El Centro: Una generación, un programa, un partido," *Diario de Costa Rica* (Mar. 15, 1944), p. 3.

for the increasing political significance of the Center had to do with the age of the members. Students who joined the Cultural Association or the Federation in the late 1930's were no longer students by 1943 and 1944. Instead, they were practicing lawyers or members of other professions. They were, in short, of an age and of a social group in which politicking would normally be expected. Consequently, it is not surprising that active participation was forthcoming at that time.[18]

Membership had increased enough to warrant a series of general conventions to decide the future political activity of the Center. A motion to initiate discussions with other groups was adopted in 1944, and within a year the Center for the Study of National Problems became a true political party. Negotiations with a like-minded organization affiliated with Leon Cortes' Democratic Party, Acción Demócrata, proved successful and on March 11, 1945, a convention of delegates from the two groups was held in the capital.

The Social Democratic Party (PSD), the PLN's direct predecessor, was initiated in this manner, and the founding of the new party properly marked the end of the first phase of National Liberation's history. The students, professors, writers, and businessmen who had participated in the various discussion groups in the late 1930's and early 1940's now became officially involved in Costa Rican partisan politics, not as social critics as they had been in the past, but as members of one of several rival political subsystems struggling to attain governmental power. Before considering the PSD, however, the second group, Democratic Action (AD), must be considered.

Democratic Action

The group that united with the Center for the Study of National Problems in order to found the Social Democratic Party was established on June 2, 1943, by leaders of Leon Cortes' Democratic Party (PD), particularly Fernando Lara. Its membership was composed of younger Cortesista activists, mostly in their

18. It is interesting to note at this point that the two centrista leaders elected to the highest positions of authority in 1944 were still among the top ranks of party leadership as this was written in 1967. They were President Daniel Oduber and Coordinator and Director of Sections Gonzalo Facio. Oduber was the National Liberation Party's presidential candidate in February, 1966, and Facio served as Ambassador to Washington during the administration of President Francisco Orlich, 1962–66.

twenties and thirties, who distributed propaganda and recruited new campaign workers. It was to have been a subsidiary
of the PD similar to the Young Republicans or Young Democrats
in the United States, but it soon came to possess an identity and
character of its own. After the 1944 election the original founders
lost interest in their creation and newer, more energetic,
persons who joined in 1944 and 1945 effectively shaped an independent political vehicle.

An energetic National Executive Council composed of Rafael
Carrillo, Alfonso Goicoechea, Francisco Jimenez, Alberto
Martén, and Eloy Morúa sped the organizational work of the
group and, using the existing Democratic Party structure as a
base, quickly organized local units in all seven provinces and
nearly two-thirds of the nation's cantons.[19] The basic unit of
organization was the cantonal assembly which met once a week
during the intense period of the 1944 campaign and was responsible for supervising party recruitment and registering voters
as well as nominating local municipal officers. Each cantonal
assembly also had an executive committee to coordinate the
weekly sessions. To judge from correspondence between cantonal and national officers during the 1943–45 period, it appears
that only the cantonal assemblies of the larger cities actually
fulfilled their obligations by meeting on a regular weekly basis.
Cantonal assemblies nominated members of their respective
provincial executive committees; all members of the seven
provincial committees, together with members of the National
Executive Committee, formed the National Executive Assembly
which was the highest day-to-day legislative organ of the organization. Yearly national conventions were held to adopt new programs, elect a five-man (later changed to seven) National Executive Committee, and nominate persons for public office.[20]

The exact reasons why Democratic Action broke away from
the Cortesista Party after the 1944 elections are not known, but
interviews with former AD leaders as well as contemporary
articles written by them indicate a general dissatisfaction with

19. From reports presented to the First Annual National Convention in
May 1944, it is known that AD had become best organized in Heredia and Ala-
juela and was poorly organized in Cartago. Archives of Acción Demócrata, San
José.

20. Acción Demócrata, "Declaración de Principios y Reglamento Interno."
Also see "Cómo funciona Acción Demócrata," Acción Demócrata (Mar. 4, 1944),
p. 1.

the excessive personalism connected with all Costa Rican parties in general and with the policies of the older leaders of the party.[21] It is known that there was a certain amount of friction between regular Cortesistas and AD leaders as early as January 1944. On January 8 a bitter intraparty struggle took place at the party's provincial nominating convention in San José when AD supported José Figueres for first position on the Cortesista list of congressional deputies.[22] Ricardo Castro Beeche, Chief of Action of the regular Cortesista Party, was in line for the position, but Figueres, in exile at the time, beat his opponent ninety-eight to sixty-five.[23] Accionistas, younger and more hotheaded than their elders, were appalled by the passive attitudes taken by older leaders regarding alleged abuses committed by Calderonista and Communist toughs; gradually they came to believe that only by becoming independent could they actively fight for their principles of reform.[24] Consequently, several days after the February 13 elections, AD formally divorced itself from the Cortesista Party and on February 26 began publishing its own weekly organ *Acción Demócrata*,[25] edited first by Alberto Martén and later by Eloy Morúa.

Since José Figueres was to play such an important role in the organization after the 1944 split with the Cortesistas, it is deemed beneficial to consider the background of the individual who later led the "War of National Liberation" and founded the National Liberation Party. Figueres was born in the village of San Ramón in the province of Alajuela on September 25, 1906, the son of a Spanish-born physician. After graduation from the Liceo de San José in 1922, he spent four years in Boston and

21. For example, see Carlos Manuel Castillo, "El Partido ideológico es necesidad en Costa Rica," *Acción Demócrata* (May 27, 1944), p. 3; (June 4, 1944), p. 4.

22. Costa Rica employs a proportional representation system of electing legislators; thus, occupying first position on a major party's list is tantamount to election.

23. See *Diario de Costa Rica* (Jan. 9, 1944), p. 1.

24. It is interesting to note that the phrase *Lucha sin Fin*, (Fight without End) was used over and over in AD propaganda of the period. It is also the name of the farm owned by José Figueres and implies that Figueres, although in exile, had a tremendous influence on the group during the formative years.

25. For a lengthy statement concerning the ostensible reasons why AD disassociated itself from the Cortesista Party together with an interesting although extremely partisan analysis of the 1944 Costa Rican political situation, see "Sensacional manifesto dirige al país 'Acción Demócrata,'" *Diario de Costa Rica* (Feb. 29, 1944), p. 1.

New York, where he read extensively from the works of Spencer.[26] Although many biographical sketches claim he graduated from the Massachusetts Institute of Technology, he actually only attended several free evening lecture courses. In 1928 he bought a small run-down farm which he renamed *La Lucha sin Fin* and devoted his interests to business until 1942 when he entered politics for the first time.

That year, 1942, marked the beginning of a six-year crisis period in Costa Rican history. Although not immediately affected by World War II, the European conflagration was felt in the small Central American republic. After Pearl Harbor, German submarines began impeding trade with the outside world, resulting in a partial economic slowdown, while tons of Anglo-American propaganda extolled the virtues of democracy and denounced authoritarianism. It was in this emotionally charged atmosphere that an American-owned fruit ship was torpedoed in Limón harbor on July 7, 1942, provoking a large anti-German riot in San José. The government was unable or unwilling to control the mob, and in the confusion business establishments (many of them owned by persons of German origin) were looted and vandalized. The Communists, in coalition with the government party at the time, viewed the disturbances as an anti-Axis popular uprising and denounced as Fascists those who criticized the ineptitude of Calderón's police. Calderón himself maintained a less extreme position, but allegedly took advantage of the chaos to intimidate political enemies. Within four days turmoil became very widespread, and Figueres, never before politically active, aroused public opinion by renting time on a local radio station to broadcast a severe critique of the Calderón government. Local newspapers carried the following advertisement:

To the Supreme Government
To residents from the allied nations
To Costa Rican citizens

We invite you to listen to a message that will be given today at 7 p.m. on radio station "America Latina" by

Don José Figueres

who will unmask the true national organization of sabotage

26. Arturo Castro Esquivel, *José Figueres Ferrer: El hombre y su obra.*

that is undermining the Republic and its international action.

San José, July 8, 1942

Francisco J. Orlich   Alberto Martén[27]

The broadcast was interrupted by the police. A voice could be heard over the still-open microphone, "By a superior order emanating from the government we are obligated to suspend this transmission."[28] Figueres continued speaking, there was a period of silence, then interlude music was heard. He was jailed for a short time before being exiled to Mexico until mid-1944.

During the early 1940's Mexico City was a hotbed of inter-hemispheric political activity and intrigue. Exiled leaders of revolutionary movements in a variety of nations used the stability and leniency of the Mexican authorities to meet together for the purpose of fomenting the cooperative overthrow of their respective governments. Out of this milieu emerged a number of ideas, programs, and organizations, among them the famed and mysterious Caribbean Legion composed of Costa Rican, Nicaraguan, Honduran, Salvadoran, Guatemalan, Dominican, and Venezuelan exiles intent on destroying the regimes of Calderón, Somoza, Carias, Hernandez Martinez, Ubico, Trujillo, and Gomez' successors. Under the circumstances, it is not surprising that this previously apolitical and unknown small businessman would undergo an almost total metamorphosis and emerge as a popular revolutionary leader. He soon acquired the political knowledge that would later enable him to lead a successful revolt—knowledge in the techniques of propaganda, subversion, and political organization. A lengthy critique of the Calderón government entitled *Palabras Gastadas* [*Wasted Words*] urged the Costa Rican citizenry to adopt more forceful methods. This approach coincided perfectly with the attitude of members of Democratic Action, and Figueres became the undisputed leader of the "hard line opposition" overnight. Almost every issue of *Acción Demócrata* contained an article or two glorifying his position,[29] and when he returned from exile on May 24,

27. Ibid., p. 26.
28. Figueres' entire speech was reprinted in *Acción Demócrata* (Mar. 4, 1944), p. 1. See also Esquivel, *José Figueres Ferrer*, p. 35.
29. See, for example, an article written by centrista Jorge Rossi, "Una visita a la Empresa San Cristóbal de José Figueres," *Acción Demócrata* (Apr. 7, 1944), p. 1.

1944, accionistas filled the streets of San José on his behalf, while women of the affiliated Fifteenth of May Movement spread flowers in his path. The editors of *Acción Demócrata* ran a special issue for the returning hero.[30]

Meanwhile, future Figueristas in both the Center for the Study of National Problems and Democratic Action had been undertaking negotiations to create a new political party. On May 15, just a few days before Figueres' triumphant return, AD had celebrated its First Annual National Convention. Two hundred delegates from all parts of the nation gave a standing ovation to a report by a special *centrista* delegation sent for the purpose of encouraging mutual cooperation. Later in the same year the two groups voted to merge. As previously noted, relations between them had always been very cordial and friendly. Leaders of the Center often gave talks and short speeches before weekly meetings of the San José cantonal assembly of AD and members of each wrote short articles for the other's publications. In a letter dated January 6, 1944, Eloy Morúa, Director of *Acción Demócrata*, had officially asked for *centrista* collaboration and assistance in his group's forthcoming periodical: "Our official organ of publicity *Acción Demócrata*, belongs, in fact, to both of our groups."[31] Alberto F. Cañas, Director of *Surco*, replied in kind by putting his monthly review "at the disposal of your group...."[32] In April the assemblies of both organizations nominated three-man teams to discuss the possibilities of combining forces. Rodrigo Facio, R. A. Zúñiga, and Mario Quirós, representing the Center, and R. A. Chavarría, Alfonso Goicoechea, and Mario Hernandez, representing AD, met on April 30 and again on May 4.

Center members demanded the formation of a completely new party with a new name and colors, although they insisted their group should enjoy certain autonomy. *Surco* would remain the new party's ideological journal, while *Acción Demócrata* would become its organ of combat. Above all, integration would have to be on an equal basis at all levels. The representatives of AD were willing to accept most of the Center's demands but preferred to *incorporate* the latter into their group rather

30. May 27, 1944.
31. Archives of Acción Demócrata, San José.
32. Letter from Alberto F. Cañas to Alberto Martén published in *Acción Demócrata* (Feb. 26, 1944), p. 2.

than *merge* the two into a new party.[33] Although representatives of the two failed to agree on every issue, the next few months saw the completion of much necessary background work, and both created liaison committees to foster cooperation. In June, July, and August an integrated committee wrote statutes for the proposed new party and the document was published, minus the sections dealing with name, colors, and insignia, in late August.[34] A platform committee reported its work in October.[35]

Although the various committees functioned well, the basic difference between the groups—whether to form a new party or simply incorporate the Center into AD—had never been resolved, and events in September 1944 almost destroyed the unification movement. Rafael Zúñiga reported to the thirty-ninth session of the Center's Executive Committee that representatives of AD had not been disposed to give equal representation to the Center,[36] and the Center's Assembly of Active Members, meeting on the 4th, adopted a resolution to inform the Executive Committee of AD that under no circumstances would it merge unless a totally *new* group (to be called either the Social Democratic Party or the Social Republican Party) were founded with a definite ideological program based on the Center's philosophy.[37] The assembly of. Democratic Action, angered by the Center's letter, drafted a retaliatory resolution saying in part: "The Executive Assembly of Acción Demócrata, considering that the fusion of the Center for the Study of National Problems with the political group Acción Demócrata would be premature in that such a fusion would

33. *Actas de la Asamblea Ejecutiva de Acción Demócrata*, April 22, 1944, and "Informe de la comisión nombrada por la Asamblea Ejecutiva para el estudio de la posible coordinación de funciones de Acción Demócrata y el Centro de Estudio para los Problemas Nacionales [sic]," Archives of Acción Demócrata, San José. Of interest in understanding the integration of the two groups are "Muy avanzadas los negociones para la fusion de los movimientos de Acción Demócrata y el Centro para el Estudio de Problemas Nacionales," *Acción Demócrata* (Apr. 7, 1944), p. 1; and "Muy avanzados los trabajos para la fusion con el Centro," *Acción Demócrata* (July 15, 1944), p. 1.
34. *Acción Demócrata* (Aug. 19, 1944), p. 1.
35. The new party's proposed platform appeared in *Acción Demócrata* (Oct. 21, 1944), p. 4.
36. *Actas oficiales del Centro para el Estudio de Problemas Nacionales*, Archives of the Center for the Study of National Problems, San José.
37. Ibid.

cause the downfall of both factions, resolves that it will not merge at the present time. . . ."[38]

Discretion prevailed, however, and in late October a compromise was reached whereby a new party with a new name would be founded although a member of AD would serve as first president. On December 12 the executive committees of both groups began holding joint sessions every week, and by the end of the month almost all necessary details had been worked out. Major announcements were issued by the executive committees jointly, and provincial and cantonal committees and assemblies began integrating. On January 15, 1945, the duties and responsibilities of all members of the new party's executive committees were defined.[39] Although it had been known since late November, 1944, that the new party's name would be the Social Democratic Party, it was not until January 21, 1945, that the joint committees adopted the title officially, subject to ratification by the forthcoming convention.[40]

It was also agreed that the convention would be attended by one-hundred delegates from each of the two and the new Executive Committee would consist of representatives from both. The final minutes of the Center for the Study of National Problems, dated February 3, 1945, state that Rodrigo Facio, Isaac Azofeifa, Mario Quirós, Alberto Zúñiga, and Carlos Monge were elected from ten nominees to occupy positions on the new Executive Council. Acción Demócrata supplied José Figueres, Antonio Peña, Francisco Orlich, and Alberto Martén.

38. Letter from Rafael Ángel Chavarría, president of the Executive Assembly of Acción Demócrata to the National Secretary of the Center for the Study of National Problems (Sept. 11, 1944), Archives of Acción Demócrata, San José.

39. Minutes of the 4th Session of the combined executive committees (Jan. 15, 1945), Archives of the Social Democratic Party, San José.

40. Minutes of the 6th Session of the joint executive committee (Jan. 29, 1945), Archives of the Social Democratic Party, San José.

3. The Social Democratic Party

HEN THE Center for the Study of National Problems and Democratic Action finally held a joint convention on March 11, 1945,[1] a fairly strong political force was created. By merging energies the total import of both groups was magnified and intensified. Before, neither could have hoped to compete in rival partisan politics; afterward, the new party competed so well that it gained control of the Costa Rican government within three short years. First, from AD the new party inherited a national structure with local committees in many of the nation's cantons plus a small corps of leaders already experienced through their involvement in the Cortesista Party. Second, the Center for the Study of National Problems provided a small cadre of young intellectuals with a social program and the rudiments of an organized ideology.

The Center of Investigations, headed by Rafael Zúñiga, took over many of the Center's former activities and for a short time maintained itself as an autonomous entity within the new party. It was dissolved within a year, however, and reinstituted

1. It is interesting to note that José Figueres gave the closing speech of the 1945 convention and based his address on the theme, "The Conquest of the Second Republic." Three years later Figueres, aided by many Social Democrats, led that conquest and founded the Second Republic of Costa Rica.

in late 1947. The monthly review, *Surco*, was adopted as the Social Democratic ideological journal but, like the Center of Investigations, was soon disbanded.[2] *Acción Demócrata*, changed by the 1947 convention to *El Social Demócrata*, continued as the PSD's organ of combat and was published weekly until 1951.

On paper, the rules for joining or affiliating with the Social Democratic Party were very strict. To simply "adhere,"[3] one had to register with a local party office and pass a vote of approval by the district committee. A somewhat more formal member was called an *afiliado*. In order to gain such status, one was supposed to be a Costa Rican citizen and an *adherente* for one year. Furthermore, he had to prove that he was over eighteen years of age and not formally affiliated with any other political party, although under certain special circumstances, minors, natives of other Central American republics, or foreigners with intentions of naturalization could also apply. Two party members had to support his application and vouch for his character. The new member then had to pledge loyalty to the party's principles, program, and ideology, to actively work in the party organization, and to contribute financially. In return, he could vote in the district and cantonal assemblies, hold party office, and be nominated for public office. During 1945 and most of 1946 these rules were followed almost to the letter because the PSD then viewed itself as a compact, elitist party of dedicated workers; later, particularly after the death of Leon Cortes, membership became somewhat more open, and the formal rigidity was increasingly ignored.

The party was hierarchial in nature. At the lowest organizational level stood the district assembly and the district com-

2. *Surco Nuevo*, a bimonthly periodical, appeared in 1963 as the official organ of the National Liberation Party's youth organization, Juventud Liberacionista.

3. During political campaigns in the past, Costa Rican parties traditionally made use of a curious device known as *Listas de Adherentes*. Publishing endorsements of famous persons has always been widespread in many countries of the world, but Costa Rica seemed to favor quantity to quality. Lists of hundreds of persons intending to vote for this or that party used to appear in newspapers or posters; the idea seemed to be to overwhelm the opposition with longer lists. However, this practice has been used very little in recent elections. In 1966 a far more common device involved a fairly long newspaper advertisement in which a single person notified all his friends that: "I, Juan Doe, have been a follower of don Fulano de Tal all my life but now intend to vote for his opposition and urge everyone to do the same." Usually, the costs of such advertisements were paid, at least in part, by the party organization.

mittee. The assembly met weekly and every member had a vote. In addition to electing committee members, the assembly nominated candidates for local office, studied local social and economic problems, and relayed information from higher party levels. The committee was composed of a president, secretary, and treasurer and acted as an executive body for the district assembly. At the cantonal level the assembly was again open to all members residing within the area. It met four times a year and was chiefly responsible for party education, training, and discipline. The cantonal committee also consisted of three members. A five-man committee existed at the provincial level, but there was no assembly. The provincial committee was elected once a year by a provincial convention and was responsible for coordinating and supervising district and cantonal organs. It had little control over individual members, but could remove district committees if just cause could be shown. The National Executive Assembly was composed of members of the National Committee plus all members of all provincial committees. It met only at the request of the National Committee or two provincial committees and had the power to call special conventions or fulfill, on a provisional basis, the duties of the National Committee. The National Assembly, in turn, was the highest executive organ of the party and subject only to the will of the National Convention. It supervised the overall work of the party, conducted investigations in cases of suspected inefficiency or misuse of party funds, and had the power to remove lower committees and expel individual members. The National Committee (also called the Executive Committee) was composed of ten members. Yearly conventions were held at both the provincial and national levels and were composed of delegates elected by the cantonal assemblies. They served two purposes: to elect the committees at their respective levels and to nominate persons for public office. The National Convention was the highest decision-making body and could reverse actions of all committees and assemblies. In addition, the National Committee selected a three-man Honor Tribunal which resolved intraparty disputes and disciplined members.

In addition to its hierarchical structure, the PSD had five functional departments as well as the Center of Investigations. The Department of Finance was in charge of developing new sources of funds, collecting monthly levies from local cantonal organizations, and collecting dues from party members and sympathizers. The Department of Organization kept the membership records, supervised provincial and cantonal committees, and was responsible for establishing new committees in all parts of the nation. The Department of Organization also coordinated the work of the Center of Investigations with other departments. Rodrigo Facio and Mario Leiva headed the Department of Propaganda, which produced several weekly radio programs over Radio Titania and Radio Voz de Costa Rica,[4] published a regular PSD weekly column in the *Diario de Costa Rica*, and issued campaign literature in all forms. The Campesino Department worked with the Department of Organization in establishing local party assemblies in rural areas and was directly responsible for implementing suggestions and programs of the Center of Investigations pertaining to the health, sanitation, and educational problems of Costa Rica's rural poor. A similar Labor Department, originally headed by Carlos Monge and José Luis Molina, was established in order to wean votes of the urban proletariat from the Calderón government. In 1947 this department established free "Popular Schools" for workers and their families.

The activities of the Social Democratic Party were necessarily limited by the newness and small size of the group, and financial difficulties were not the least of its problems. The treasurer's report for fiscal year 1945–46 stated that such problems did exist: "Upon assuming the treasury on April 4, 1945 . . . or, as it were, a little more than a month after the foundation of the party, the economic situation was not satisfactory and the prospects were uncertain."[5] Although available membership lists for mid-1945 are incomplete, one may obtain an idea of the smallness of the party shortly after its establishment by a letter from Alberto Martén to Eugenio Rodriguez dated April 9, 1945. Martén, Secretary of Organization, certified 282 affiliates in San

4. The Saturday night program "Onda Libre" over Radio Titania often presented Social Democratic opinions and attitudes through a popular Mr. Dooley-like character called Juan Pueblo. Juan, who talked in the typical dialect of the Costa Rican peasant, conducted dialogues with many contemporary political leaders.

5. Partido Social Demócrata, "Informe Anual de tesorería Período 1° Marzo 1945 a 30 Abril 1946," Archives of the Social Democratic Party, San José. During the first year of organization, total monthly income only averaged about $215 (U.S.). Five years later, although the party had more than tripled in membership, monthly income had not quite doubled.

José.[6] Since the PSD was strongest in the capital, the national figure could not have been more than double, and it never attracted more than 1,200 before it was incorporated into the PLN in the early 1950's.[7] The slow growth rate was due to the fact that the party could never shake its image as a closed group of liberal intellectuals. Although repeated attempts were made to incorporate the Costa Rican masses, the party never attracted much popular following as a 1948 editorial in *El Social Demócrata* admitted. Answering criticisms that the party would not do well in the election for a Constituent Assembly after the 1948 revolution, the leadership replied that the outcome, from an ideological point of view, would really make no difference: "How, then, can our party go to the elections with its own forces. Some people say that we are only 1% of the electorate, and that nobody knows about us nor pays us any attention. That does not matter: we are going to undertake a permanent task of public education, and that task we will accomplish on our own account. The numerical results of the election do not bother us much. In any event, perhaps we will obtain something more than 1%."[8]

The new party was unquestionably hurt by Figueres' sudden resignation less than a month after the founding convention. An important national political figure by 1945, Figueres was undisputed leader of the youngest and most militant anti-Calderonistas within the country; as such his membership was highly valued by the PSD which direly needed publicity. Although some irregularities later turned up in the Finance Department, which he headed from March 11 to April 14, 1945, Figueres formally cited "petty jealousies" within the PSD's leadership ranks as his reasons for departure.[9] Nevertheless, his break with the group did not prevent close collaboration between the future president and important PSD activists during the next few years. As a general rule Social Democrats proved to be Figueres' most steadfast supporters.

6. Archives of the Social Democratic Party, San José.
7. Ibid.
8. *El Social Demócrata* (July 3, 1948), p. 4. As predicted, the Social Democrats received an insignificant 6,415 votes and did even worse in the contest for permanent legislative deputies the following year, obtaining 5,169 votes.
9. Minutes of the National Executive Committee of the Social Democratic Party (Apr. 14, 1948), Archives of the Social Democratic Party, San José. In 1949 Figueres told a Spanish reporter he had resigned from the party because he needed to spend much time out of the country. See *La Prensa Libre* (Apr. 2, 1949), p. 1.

Numerically small and lacking both financial and popular support, the neophyte Social Democratic Party was obliged to seek strength in coalition with larger antigovernment parties and was instrumental in creating a united opposition for the 1946 congressional elections.[10] Consequently, during the autumn of 1945 a makeshift alliance, formally entitled the Democratic Union Party, was pieced together from Otilio Ulate's National Union Party (PUN), Leon Cortes' Democratic Party, and the PSD. A January 1946 convention of the antigovernment coalition subsequently chose PSD President Peña Chavarría and Director of Propaganda Rodrigo Facio to occupy first and sixth places, respectively, on the San José provincial list of deputies. Francisco Orlich was chosen to occupy the opposition's third position in the province of Alajuela.[11]

The February 1946 congressional elections were a sort of dress rehearsal for the 1948 presidential struggle, which ended in civil war. The government won and the opposition charged fraud, insisting that voting identity cards were taken unlawfully, votes were burned, opposition party members were threatened, and Communist strong men influenced voters at the polls.[12]

The united opposition suffered a setback when Leon Cortes, who had been serving as chief of the coalition, died on March 3. Leaderless, the three parties began quarreling and for several months it appeared that the national coalition would disintegrate. It was held together, however, by a common enemy in the form of the Calderón-Picado-Mora government, which was unquestionably stronger than any of the antigovernment parties individually. A new National Executive Committee of the Opposition was convoked in June 1946, and the Social Democratic Party nominated Francisco Orlich and Carlos Luis Valverde to represent it. Several months later the PSD Executive Committee passed a resolution declaring support for a united convention in which all parties, regardless of size, would be free

10. "Urge crear un gran frente único de reivindicación," *Acción Demócrata* (June 16, 1945), p. 1. Also see "Es urgente un frente unido de la oposición," *Acción Demócrata* (Sept. 1, 1945), p. 2.

11. Peña was later asked to resign his position in the party because he refused to relinquish his legislative seat after the combined opposition resolved to boycott the national legislature.

12. Arturo Castro Esquivel, *José Figueres Ferrer: El hombre y su obra*, p. 26.

to choose their own delegates and would be represented equally.[13]

The Executive Committee of the opposition decided on November 15, 1946, to establish an organizing commission which would make arrangements for a Grand National Convention on February 13, 1947. The commission was composed of Marcial Rodriguez and Mario Echandi from the National Union Party, Ricardo Beeche and Eladio Trejos from the Democratic Party, Eloy Morúa and Carlos Monge Alfaro from the Social Democratic Party, and José Figueres and Roberto Salazar Mata from the Authentic Cortesista Party.[14] The Grand National Convention ultimately chose National Unionist Otilio Ulate as "Chief of the National Opposition" and official opposition candidate for president in the forthcoming election to be held on February 8, 1948.[15] Figueres was elected Chief of Action, a position which enabled him to accumulate much power.

It must be emphasized that members of the opposition, as individuals, remained divided into three discernible schools of thought regarding policy toward the Calderón-Picado-Mora government during this period. These schools closely approximated partisan loyalties, although considerable overlapping existed. The first, led by Fernando Castro Cervantes, included a majority of older, more conservative Cortesistas and favored a policy of cooperating with Calderón in order to lessen the government's reliance on the Communists. The second, led by Ulate, favored continuous opposition but only by legal methods. This group, which included the bulk of PUN activists, believed the government would honor a pledge to permit free elections. Figueres and his followers in the third school saw no possibility of defeating the Calderón regime short of armed revolt and were willing to overthrow it by violence. Undoubtedly, most Social Democrats, still in their twenties and thirties, favored a less cautious approach than their elders. A speech by Figueres on

13. See "La formación de un 'Frente Unido Oposicionista' ha sido planteada por el Partido Social Demócrata," *Acción Demócrata* (Sept. 21, 1946), p. 1.

14. After Figueres resigned from the Social Democratic Party in April 1945, he returned to the Democratic Party of Leon Cortes. After Cortes' death in March 1946, a rift widened in the leadership circles of the party, and several months later Figueres and Otto Cortes, son of the old chieftain, formed the splinter party mentioned above. It remained very small and worked closely with the Social Democratic Party.

15. An especially informative account of opposition maneuvers during this period can be found in *Acción Demócrata* (May 6, 1947).

August 22, 1946, urging armed revolt was widely applauded by the PSD.[16]

Although Figueres' militants were unquestionably the weakest of the three schools for the time, the summer of 1947 witnessed a series of antigovernment riots that strengthened their hand. On Sunday, July 20, the famous Huelga de Brazos Caídos (Strike of the Folded Arms) began in Cartago, and police attacked the crowd, injuring several persons. Monday, the Federation of University Students voted to join the protest, and the following day a large crowd gathered in front of Ulate's *Diario de Costa Rica*, where Figueres demanded the overthrow of the government. On Wednesday students marched through the streets demanding that shopkeepers close their doors. Employees of the San José banks struck and the business community was paralyzed. On August 2 several hundred women of various social classes, led by schoolteacher Emma Gamboa, staged a parade which culminated in a demonstration in San José's national park across from the presidential palace. In addition to normal governmental suppression of these acts, the opposition later charged that Communist Popular Vanguard strong-arm men had attacked and terrorized individual citizens.[17]

Ulate, following his stated policy of legally contesting the regime, had attempted to insure governmental noninterference in the electoral process by signing a Pact of Honor with the National Republican candidate, Calderón Guardia. By the terms of the pact, both sides agreed to respect the judgment of the National Electoral Tribunal and to refrain from violence and other illegal procedures. The campaign, which lasted from early 1947 to February 1948, was a particularly bitter one and both sides claimed fraud and illegal campaigning. After the ballots were counted Ulate had apparently won by 10,000 votes, but the government formally appealed to the National Tribunal. On February 28 the Tribunal declared Ulate the victor, 54,931 to 44,438, but a holdover Legislative Assembly declared the elections invalid within a week. A wave of protest

16. It is obvious that many Social Democrats favored the more forceful methods of Figueres over the relatively mild ones of Ulate. A letter from Eloy Morúa, secretary general of the PSD, to Ulate, dated September 10, 1947, urged the opposition to adopt the methods of "continuous strikes such as the Huelga de Brazos Caídos, the organization of sabotage, and the training of the citizenry for armed action," Archives of the Social Democratic Party, San José.

17. See "Otro triunfo del pueblo," *El Social Demócrata* (Aug. 11, 1947), p. 1.

broke out among supporters of the opposition, and the violence that had characterized the campaign was renewed. Sensing a direct threat to their security, governmental leaders began jailing political rivals; consequently, the situation deteriorated — law and order broke down in the capital and major cities.

However, it was not until March 8 that the crisis reached a climax. National political traditions were broken when an order was issued to arrest Ulate. Although the president-elect managed to escape, the police killed a close political associate and civil war began.

On March 10 Figueres gathered a small group and began an armed revolt from La Lucha.[18] The short war that followed lasted only six weeks and was fought on two major fronts. The first, in the mountainous region south of the Meseta Central, involved a series of battles on Figueres' farm, the village of San Isidro del General, and in the region that separates the General Valley from the Pacific Ocean in the province of Puntarenas. Battles were also fought in El Empalme and in the small village of San Isidro de la Muerta, just south of the city of Cartago. The northern front involved guerrilla warfare in the mountainous region that extends to the north of the province of Alajuela, mostly in the cantons of San Ramón and San Carlos. In addition to the two major fronts, isolated battles took place in the cities of Cartago and Limón. By April 20 the Picado government sent representatives to discuss peace terms, and Figueres' triumphant army marched into the national capital four days later.[19]

Although the revolution had been fought in order to protect Ulate's victory, he was not allowed to assume the presidency for a year and a half. Instead, Figueres appointed himself president of a revolutionary government, the Founding Junta of the Second Republic, and ruled by decree for eighteen months. During that period he instituted a number of innovations that have been the subject of heated partisan controversy ever since. Communism was outlawed as a political force in the nation, and the Communist-oriented labor unions were destroyed,

18. Between 1945 and 1948 Figueres had been receiving weapons and ammunition through friends in Mexico.

19. See *La Guerra de la Liberación 1948*. Also useful in analyzing the 1948 revolution is a special eleven-page history of the war in *La República* (Mar. 11, 1951), pp. 17–28.

weakened, or replaced by pro-Western workers' groups. The entire banking industry was nationalized, and the various banks operating within the nation became government-owned corporations. The army was permanently abolished and replaced by a policelike Civil Guard. A number of loan and assistance programs were implemented to provide small rural landowners greater credit facilities. Social security laws, laws dealing with a myriad of guarantees including minimum wage benefits, rights of tenure, free or low-cost hospitalization, maternity care, and child support payments, were actively enforced for the first time. Finally, the nation's electoral machinery was totally revamped, and a nonpartisan Supreme Tribunal of Elections was established to oversee a professional permanent staff of employees.

Whether one views these changes as meaningful reforms or political chicanery depends entirely on partisan loyalty. Staunch Figueristas insist that checking Communist strength has tended to insure the growth and institutionalization of democratic political institutions. As proof they point to the chaotic days of 1942–48 when Communist toughs were given carte blanche freedom to molest supporters of the Opposition. Similarly, they argue that the banks, often foreign-owned, were previously operated for the exclusive benefit of the wealthy. Common people (*el pueblo*) had never been able to borrow money for capital investment; hence, the old banking industry insured ever-greater stratification of the social hierarchy. An institutionalized armed military force, they maintain, was simply not needed in a relatively tranquil and isolated nation like Costa Rica; furthermore, it represented a drain on the federal treasury, and its very existence was a constant threat to civilian government. Loan programs and social security measures have been defended on the basis of humanitarianism and social integration. Figueres' supporters insist that the once-deprived social classes have since maintained a genuine stake in society and its governmental structures.

On the other hand, anti-Figueristas offer convincing arguments that the work of the 1948–49 revolutionary government was not nearly so noble. First, there is the persistent and obvious fact that Figueres and his friends had absolutely *no legal right* to govern in 1948–49. A new president, Ulate, had been freely elected, a war had been fought to protect his mandate, and the nation had become tranquil within days after the surrender of the Calderón forces. Therefore, Figueres' assumption of power was a violation of both the letter and spirit of the Constitution. Second, many suspect that by undermining Communist strength Figueres merely eliminated an additional political foe. Moreover, there is a strong feeling among Costa Rican liberals that the Popular Vanguard Party, led since its creation by its widely respected founder, Manuel Mora, has never fit the usual stereotype of the Latin American Communist organization. Also, many point to the undeniable fact that young Communist toughs were not the only ones who were guilty of harrassment during the 1942–48 period; opponents of the Calderón–Picado–Mora government had also been guilty of taking to the streets and employing the same tactics. Third, Figueres' opponents insist that by nationalizing the Costa Rican banking industry, friends of the Founding Junta were guaranteed an abundance of low-interest, long-term loans. Besides, many feel that nationalization generally decreased efficiency by removing the element of competition. Fourth, the army, rather than being abolished, was merely replaced by an equal-sized Civil Guard that has looked about the same, behaved about the same, and functioned about the same as the old armed force. Critics maintain that the only thing changed was the name of the organization; some believe it was only a clever device to give legal status to leaders of Figueres' Army of National Liberation, who soon assumed positions of authority in the Civil Guard. Fifth, the loan and assistance programs have been described as cynical attempts to "purchase" the votes of the rural poor by some, and have been criticized for lack of effectiveness by others. Anti-Figueristas correctly assert that social security and minimum wage laws were originally promulgated during Calderón Guardia's presidential administration in the early 1940's but *could not be implemented at that time due to Ulatista and Cortesista opposition.* Therefore, they argue that credit for these reforms should be given to Calderón, not Figueres. Finally, an additional criticism of the Founding Junta has haunted the National Liberation Party for two decades. Figueres' government voted the appropriation of public funds in order to compensate those whose homes, farms, and businesses had been destroyed during the 1948 war. Yet, anti-Figueres elements insist that supporters of the former (Calderón) government were treated unfairly, while friends of the Junta were awarded generous settlements. There have been persistent charges, for example, that the bill Figueres collected for damages to his farm "La Lucha sin Fin" was considerably higher than the immediate prewar value of the property. Spokesmen for the Founding Junta deny these charges of wrongdoing.

The only major innovation that has received nearly universal public support is the electoral reform. Nearly all citizens, regardless of partisan loyalties, agree that voting has been more honest since the war. Still, anti-Figueristas tend to credit the professional administrators employed by the Supreme Tribunal of Elections for the increased honesty, whereas Figueres' supporters place greater emphasis and reward on those who established the present Tribunal in the first place.

The various charges and countercharges have so clouded the political waters that an objective appraisal of the accomplishments of the Founding Junta of the Second Republic would involve an enormous task not within the scope of this study. What is important for our purposes, however, is the influence, prestige, and power that the small Social Democratic Party was able to acquire as a result of Figueres' assumption of governmental power. Since many Social Democrats had been Figueres' most steadfast supporters as well as his closest friends, both before and during the revolution, the Founding Junta contained PSD members in a proportion far greater than their strength in the nation. Gonzalo Facio became Minister of Justice; Francisco Orlich, Minister of Public Works; Uladislao Gamez, Minister of Public Education; Bruce Masís, Minister of Agriculture and Industries; and Dr. Raul Blanco, Minister of Public Health. Father Benjamín Nuñez, although not formally a PSD member because of his position in the labor movement, had been a close collaborator for several years and was appointed Minister of Labor. In addition, Rafael Chavarría was named Administrator of the National Liquor Factory; Rafael Angel Álvarez became auditor of the Department of Prisons and Reformatories; Eloy Morúa became Chief of the National Office of Information, and Eugenio Rodriguez was appointed Director of Radio Coordination. Undoubtedly, the close ties that had existed between the president of the Founding Junta and the Social Democratic Party had benefited both.

Although Figueres and Ulate had been allies during the 1948

political campaign, personal and political relations between them had never been close, and Figueres' assumption of power after the war separated the two into permanent mutual hostility and drove a wedge between each of their respective groups of followers. As a result, the PSD, which had always maintained cordial relations with Ulate, attempting for a time to bridge the ever-widening gap between the two leaders, ultimately lined up behind Figueres. Yet, the process of alienation from Ulate was a slow one. The PSD Executive Committee voted on July 13, 1948 to participate in the elections for the Constituent Assembly alone, rather than in coalition, and also to refrain from criticizing any party or individual during the campaign.[20] Furthermore, a special nominating convention on October 17 passed a resolution to support (1) Ulate's right to assume the presidency and (2) Figueres' right to continue his revolutionary junta.[21] Social Democratic propaganda during the campaign carried photographs of Figueres and Ulate and praised both leaders equally. On the surface it appeared that the former anti-Calderonista forces were still friendly and cordial. Such, however, was not the case. As early as July, Mario Echandi, number two man in the National Union Party organization, had publicly stated that the PSD was working to impede the succession of Ulate.[22] A letter from Ulate to the Executive Committee of the Social Democratic Party dated September 1, 1948, further testifies to the growing rift between the PSD and the president-elect.[23] That split became complete as a result of an editorial published in *El Social Demócrata* on October 16. Hinting that other parties might not be too democratic, the editorial stated in part: "But the Social Democratic nominees will not be determined by seventy persons, as in other parties, but by a numerous and authentic Popular Convention in which all delegates will have full opportunity to express their thoughts, their anxieties, and

20. Letter from Carlos José Gutierrez, secretary general of the Social Democratic Party, to members of the San José provincial committee (July 14, 1948), Archives of the Social Democratic Party, San José.

21. Although an explanation of the detailed proceedings of the revolutionary government are out of the scope of this study, its most notable accomplishments were the substitution of the old army by a new Public Force, the nationalization of the entire Costa Rican banking system, promulgation of a new Constitution, and the outlawing of the Communist Party.

22. "Audaz mentira anda divulgando D. Mario Echandi," *El Social Demócrata* (July 31, 1948), p. 1.

23. Archives of the Social Democratic Party, San José.

criticisms." Taking the editorial as an insult, Ulate wrote another letter to the PSD Executive Committee on the 17th refusing to attend the PSD's convention.[24] By December followers of Ulate were openly calling the PSD the "Official Party," thus invoking livid memories of Calderón days as well as using a clever form of innuendo to compare Figueres to Calderón. The Social Democrats agitated opposition discord even more. In addition to the editorial mentioned above, a letter signed by all members of the National Executive Committee and all provincial committees, dated August 20, 1948,[25] and another from the Executive Committee alone, later republished in *El Social Demócrata*,[26] exhibited the same attitude as the letters of Ulate.

The more strained relations became between the PSD and Ulate, the closer they became between the PSD and Figueres. Treasury records for 1948 show Figueres' agricultural and industrial firm, S.A.I. San Cristobal, Ltda., contributed $821.50 (U.S) to the Social Democratic Party in September.[27] Social Democratic handbills and posters printed for the 1949 legislative elections carried large photographs of Figueres alone, whereas similar campaign literature for the Constituent Assembly several months earlier had supported Ulate and Figueres equally. During the 1949 campaign paid advertisements boasted: "The Social Democratic Party is the only party that has promised the people to defend the revolutionary work of the government of Don José Figueres Ferrer."

By mid-1949 the breach between the revolutionary government and Ulate was complete. José Figueres explains the break in terms of Ulate's mistrust. The latter never believed that the Founding Junta would return the presidency and attacked much of the revolutionary government's program for that reason. According to Figueres, Ulate's closest advisors, particularly Mario Echandi, took advantage of Ulate's mistrust by constantly preying upon his fears in order to widen the rift and thereby assure positions for themselves in the forthcoming administration.[28]

Although the Social Democratic Party technically existed

24. Ibid.
25. Ibid.
26. (Sept. 4, 1948), p. 1.
27. Archives of the Social Democratic Party, San José. Colones were converted into United States dollars at the then current rate of 5.60 to 1.
28. Interview with José Figueres (Mar. 29, 1966).

until early 1954, it was merged into the new National Liberation Party after 1950. Beginning in January 1950, several months after Figueres turned the government over to Ulate, informal discussions between leaders of the revolutionary movement were conducted concerning the foundation of a new party. By early 1951 Social Democratic leaders were spending most of their time organizing the PLN. The PSD, for all practical purposes, ceased to exist, although the fiction of a separate party structure was maintained for legal reasons. In most cases, the leaders of both parties were the same persons, but great care was taken to present separate lists to the Electoral Registry to gain legal recognition for both.

As a result of the 1948 war José Figueres became a charismatic national caudillo overnight. Wherever he went crowds gathered to "viva don Pepe." This widespread personal following cut across regional, class, and family lines and provided the PLN with a national hero. The Social Democratic Party supplied a leadership cadre with a reasonably well-defined platform and ideology; Figueres was now in a position to supply the mass support the PSD had never been able to attract. Together the two took advantage of the crisis period of the decade of transition and forged a new type of political organization—the permanent political party. Although the National Liberation Party was the first of the large contemporary parties to become institutionalized, all groups have had to become more highly structured, if for no other reason than to compete in the political struggle. Both the National Union Party of Otilio Ulate and the National Republican Party of R. A. Calderón Guardia have changed drastically since the 1940's. The day when "parties" simply fastened the suffix "ista" to the name of their candidates is long since over.

As a final postscript to this chapter it is interesting to note that Costa Rica almost had another "Social Democratic Party" in conjunction with the 1970 presidential election. José Figueres threatened to turn his back on his own political creation if the PLN machinery failed to openly support him. In 1968 he declared that a new party would be founded employing the 1945–53 name. His subsequent nomination, however, precluded an open split within liberacionista ranks and the formation of yet another Figuerista political organization.

4. Establishment of the Party

D URING the 1948 revolution Figueres, his lieutenants, and
leaders of the Social Democratic Party began considering
the possibilities of founding a new doctrinaire political
party based on the PSD ideals of social reform. No action was
taken immediately after the armistice, however, because the
activities of the Founding Junta of the Second Republic took
much time and energy. But as relations between Figueres and
Ulate worsened, the motivation to establish a new political
machine grew greater. The poor showing made by the Social
Democrats in the elections of 1948 and 1949 further convinced
leaders of the revolutionary government that a completely new
organization would have to be built around the charismatic
personality of Figueres. Consequently, three weeks after
turning the presidency over to Ulate a series of meetings were
held in the homes of Figueres and Orlich. Although very
informal, the meetings between January 1950 and October 1951
laid the groundwork for what was to eventually become the PLN.[1]

1. Most of the data in this section were obtained by interviews with party
leaders active during the period under consideration. No minutes or records
were kept in those early meetings.

One of the major items of contention concerned the method to be employed when establishing local party units in rural areas. Although Figueres was known as a popular hero among anti-Calderonistas in all parts of the nation, neither he nor the Social Democratic Party could count on organized support below the provincial capitals and other centers of population. One group believed completely new local committees should be formed, composed of persons not previously involved in politics. A second group would have cultivated the support of cantonal and provincial caciques (regional leaders or political bosses with personalist groups of followers) who had not had reputations as Calderonistas. A compromise was finally reached whereby new committees would be formed whenever possible and caciques would only be used in very remote areas where new organizational structure would be impractical. The only regional leader with more than a village or cantonal following asked to join the new party was Dr. Hernan Vargas Vargas, whose personalist movement was fairly well established throughout the province of Guanacaste. Dr. Vargas was offered control of the new party in his province, but he refused because he believed independent action offered greater benefits to his people.[2]

The National Liberation Movement[3]

The distinction between the National Liberation *Party* and the National Liberation *Movement* must be made at this point. Although no formal organization existed between the 1948 war and October 1951 when the Fundamental Charter of the new party was signed at La Paz, Francisco Orlich's ranch,[4] Figueres and his friends, including many PSD leaders, already referred to themselves jointly as the National Liberation Movement.

2. Interview with Dr. Vargas (Apr. 14, 1966).
3. The term "movement" actually had two completely different connotations between 1948 and 1953. In the broader sense the National Liberation Movement referred collectively to supporters of Figueres' National Liberation Army during the civil war. In the narrow sense it referred to the closed, semisecret group of leaders that established the National Liberation Party. To avoid confusion only the second connotation is employed in subsequent pages.
4. José Figueres explains that the Fundamental Charter was originally to have been entitled La Carta de La Paz (The Charter of Peace) after the ranch on which it was signed. That name was not adopted, however, due to the contemporary strength of McCarthyism in the United States. The leaders who drafted the charter were afraid it might be misconstrued as a Communist-inspired program because the Soviet line was emphasizing "world peace" in those years. Interview with José Figueres (Mar. 29, 1966).

After 1951 the term "Movement" was retained to include only the small, secretive group of select leaders that founded the "party." The Movement was, in effect, a combined board of directors and "Establishment," in the British sense, which served—in the words of Gonzalo Facio—as the "ideological director of the party."[5] Few party members outside the inner circle even knew of its presence. New members were required to pass a unanimous vote, consequently the Movement never exceeded thirty-two.[6] Although this group of leaders had been meeting on an irregular basis since January 1950, formal convocations of the Plenary Council did not begin until December 19, 1951, about two months after the Fundamental Charter was drafted.

The fundamental nature of the movement to the party was clearly emphasized on page 15 (the final page) of the original Fundamental Charter, which stated in part:

> In order to fight for the liberty of the Costa Rican citizen, and in accord with the concepts and aspirations defined in this document, a political-social movement is established with the name of THE NATIONAL LIBERATION MOVEMENT.
>
> The fundamental ideas and plans of the Movement shall be put before the body-politic for examination so that a national conscience of support might arise which shall ultimately arrive at practical solutions to national problems proposed by the NATIONAL LIBERATION MOVEMENT.

The above clauses were stricken from subsequent editions and many persons in positions of party trust in the 1960's assume that the "National Liberation Movement"—a term which occasionally appeared in conjunction with early party propaganda as a synonym for the "National Liberation Party"—was simply a first name that was subsequently changed.

Due to the small membership of the movement, its structural organization was quite simple. The Plenary Council was

5. Minutes of Plenary Council of the National Liberation Movement (Aug. 29, 1953).

6. Original members were Raul Blanco, Rodrigo Facio, Gonzalo Facio, José Figueres, Bruce Masís, Luis Alberto Monge, Benjamín Nuñez, Daniel Oduber, Francisco J. Orlich, Mario Quirós, Jorge Rossi, Gonzalo Solórzano, Fidel Tristán, Fernando Valverde, Fernando Volio, Armando Arauz, and Alfonso Carro. Uladislao Humberto Pacheco, Rafael Carrillo, and Carlos José Gutierrez were sworn in several months after the organization was founded.

composed of active members and required a two-thirds quorum. It met every two months although meetings became less and less frequent toward the end of the group's existence as a body separate from the party. Officially it was charged with possessing "the character of Supreme Authority on all points of ideology and its practical application. . . ."[7] It elected its own presiding officer who was called "chief of the movement" and approved (by unanimous vote) all candidates for membership. In addition to its duties concerning party ideology, the movement also served as a final judge on questions concerning party organization and (at least in the beginning) party discipline. José Figueres served as chief throughout the entire history of the movement and through that position exercised effective control over the emerging party organization.

In order to develop a clear statement of party ideology and programs, separate committees of no less than five movement members were established to deal with the following areas: banking, Caribbean economic affairs, electricity, health, public works, history of the War of Liberation, juridical affairs, university affairs, and municipal affairs. The chairmen of the committees, plus the chief of the movement, formed the Directory, whose president was Raul Blanco. He served as the number two man and presided over the meeting of the Plenary Council in absence of the chief. The Directory met every Wednesday (although, like the Plenary Council, meetings became sporadic towards the end) and coordinated the labors of the committees.

The National Liberation Movement ceased functioning in March 1955 for several reasons. First, with political victory in 1953, much of the former militancy that had pushed National Liberation leaders to work so fervently had worn thin. The pressure to maintain a tightly knit, unified structure was no longer felt, and movement members were less inclined to attend regular meetings. Second, many members were serving in the Figueres government and had little free time to pursue their former interests. Third, by the 1954–55 period the National Liberation Party had become firmly established and the movement simply duplicated the work of the party's National Directory in many ways. The same persons were involved in both organizations, the same ideas were discussed, and much

7. Fundamental Charter of the National Liberation Movement (1st printing).

needless repetition developed. Fourth, the party had grown enormously, and new persons – persons not included in the "inner circle" – had already attained positions of leadership. The movement, because of its unanimity clause, did not exactly coincide with the changing leadership structure of the party, so a certain amount of embarrassment developed when information concerning its existence leaked to the press following a difference of opinion between Fernando Valverde and Alfonso Giocoechea. Although the Movement was never formally disbanded, meetings of the Plenary Council and the Directory became less and less regular and were finally discontinued altogether.

It was noted in chapter 3 that the machinery of the Social Democratic Party was used as a basis for the new party structure. Care was taken, however, to maintain the legal fiction of two separate organizations between early 1952 and mid-1954. According to law a formal petition containing signatures of qualified voters in all seven provinces had to be presented to the Civil Registry in order to gain legal recognition,[8] and the honor of being the first to sign went to Julia Fernandez de Cortes, widow of the former president. This act was intended to gain the PLN two advantages. First, it appealed to women and symbolized National Liberation's support for feminine suffrage, an innovation of the Constitution of 1949; and, second, it gained the support of former Cortesistas. The petition was presented to the Civil Registry on May 5, 1952. Once the new party was legalized, elections for the Executive Committee were held by a hastily gathered national convention; Francisco Orlich was elected president, Gonzalo Solórzano became secretary general, and Mario Esquivel became treasurer. Figueres was unanimously nominated presidential candidate.

More important than the newly established formal PLN machinery, however, was the silent but serious labor of the movement. Orlich, as chairman of the latter's political committee, was directly responsible for establishing units at provincial, cantonal, and local levels. Since the Social Democratic Party had maintained structures only in the more populated urban areas, new organizations had to be established in rural places, local leaders had to be recruited and trained, and party

8. The Movement appointed Gonzalo Solórzano to head the committee responsible for obtaining the necessary number of adherents.

propaganda had to be distributed in all corners of the national territory. Although the Fundamental Charter specifically stipulated that members of local committees had to be elected, the political committee often appointed officers in remote areas. From reports of the political committee it is apparent that this work progressed most rapidly in Alajuela and most slowly in Puntarenas.[9] By August 1952, the party was established in all cantons plus 82 per cent of all districts and had a monthly income of $6,900 (U.S.) with another $75,000 worth of pledges.

As a postscript to the separate history of the movement, the concept was partially reinstituted following electoral defeat in 1966. Ideological cleavages between liberal and conservative, between young and old, had become so deep that the party's top officials, particularly Figueres, again felt it necessary to establish dialogue between formal and informal leaders outside the confines and rigidity of the regular organs and committees. Consequently, a series of "new movement" meetings were held with greatly expanded "membership." Much of the old homogeneity, community of interests, and esprit de corps that had characterized the earlier movement was lacking, however, and little was done to seriously cope with intraparty problems.

Three major factors hampered the new movement's effectiveness. First, relationships between individuals were different; the old movement had been a small clique of close friends, all about the same age, who had worked together for nearly a decade, won a war by fighting side by side in combat, and gained similar governmental experience as a result of their involvement with the Founding Junta. However, such was not the case with the new movement. A double generation gap separated some of the participants. Older leaders, many of them in their sixties, seldom maintained close personal contact with younger leaders, some in their twenties. Younger leaders shared little of the camaraderie engendered by mutual sacrifice in 1948; likewise, older leaders failed to recognize or appreciate the New Leftist ideas that united the youths. Figueres and his generation had sought to emulate Franklin Roosevelt and Haya de la Torre; younger Liberacionistas were more influenced by Herbert Marcuse and Albert Camus. Second, the original movement came into being when public enthusiasm was evident and

9. Archives of the National Liberation Party, San José.

Liberacionismo was at its peak; its reinstitutionalized descendant attempted to function immediately after an embarrassing
defeat at the polls when morale was at an all-time low. Third,
intraparty intrigue over the selection of the 1970 presidential
candidate was so intense that the new movement was viewed
with considerable suspicion. Rodrigo Carazo, a bright economist
in his mid-forties and president of the Costa Rican legislature
at the time, was waging a determined and bitter campaign for
the nomination against his long-time mentor, José Figueres.
Also, the left wing of the party was in open rebellion. The leftist
intellectuals of the Patio de Agua Group[10] and leaders of the PLN
Youth were urging Alfonso Carro, former Minister of Labor in
Orlich's administration, to make a bid against Figueres. Hence,
both groups tended to view the new movement as a pro-Figueres
power play.

Recruitment

The young professionals of the generation of '48 (i.e., the
leaders of the Social Democratic Party plus Figueres and his
lieutenants) sought to construct a completely new political

10. The PLN's left wing—Benjamín Nuñez, Alfonso Carro, Fernando Volio,
most leaders of the Youth organization, and others—had exhausted themselves
trying to elect Daniel Oduber in 1966. After his defeat they blamed the party's
conservatives for "foot dragging"; the rightists, then led (more or less) by former
President Francisco Orlich, in turn let it be known that they would not tolerate
a second Oduber candidacy in 1970. As a result, an open split occurred, and the
leftists began meeting in Nuñez' home, "Patio de Agua" near Coronado. The
result of those separate caucuses was the Declaration of Patio de Agua, a highly
socialist document, demanding, among other things, nationalization of basic
industries, large-scale land reform, and severe restrictions on foreign-based
(i.e., American-based) enterprises. Moderates in the party attempted to ignore it,
conservatives were outraged, and Figueres, already having declared himself
the next presidential candidate, broke his tradition as Great Conciliator by
labeling it the "work of madmen," thus alienating his former companions and
supporters on the left as well as the entire membership of the PLN Youth. Orlich's
subsequent death further tended to clothe Figueres in the mantle of conservative
leadership.
    Oduber also lost the goodwill of his former admirers. As the most recent
presidential candidate he controlled the party machinery more than any other
single individual (except, perhaps, Figueres himself), and the left looked to him
for leadership. His surprise decision to support Figueres—and thus guarantee
Figueres' nomination over Rodrigo Carazo, a moderate, or a fellow leftist such
as Carro—pulled the political pins out from under the Patio de Agua Group and
left it debilitated. Some key leftist leaders unenthusiastically supported Figueres
in 1970 for reasons of party loyalty; others turned their backs on the PLN. As this
is written, the possibilities of a new offshoot party being formed in the foreseeable
future appear great.

vehicle based on social elements not previously active in politics. According to PLN propaganda, they sought to bring the common man into the political life of the nation, to enable him to take an active part, and to give him a direct stake in governmental decision-making. If this was the case, it seems reasonable to assume that individuals recruited to fill local leadership positions after 1951 would be socially mobile persons from the lower-middle and lower classes who entered politics as a means of bettering their relative positions. They would also be expected to be more traditionally oriented than the original founders, less interested in politics at the time of entering the party, less ideological, more religious, and more authoritarian.[11]

TABLE 1

PERIOD OF
RECRUITMENT

Year	Per Cent
1956–66	34.0
1951–55	50.5
1940–50	15.5
Total	100.0
(n)	(103)

The first item to be considered involves the present rank of the post-1951 recruits. Since positions of national party leadership were originally filled by members of the generation of '48, it can be hypothesized *that those leaders recruited after 1951 still occupy local party positions in the mid-1960's in relation to the founders.* This hypothesis was tested by tabulating three sets of leaders, those who joined before 1951 (the founders), those who joined between 1951 and 1955 (the original recruits), and those who joined in conjunction with the 1958 campaign or later (late recruits) against the three established ranks: national leaders, liaison leaders,[12] and local leaders. Table 1 breaks the leaders down by length of partisan activity.

11. To test these hypotheses as well as those in chapter 5, a sample of 103 leaders or former leaders was interviewed at length by the author between December 1965 and June 1966. Selection methods, an English translation of the questionnaire, coding procedures, and marginal distributions can be found in the appendix.

12. The term "liaison leader" will be applied to all those who at the time of interview were deemed to occupy an intermediate position in the party. They

Table 2 demonstrates that three-fourths of the founders are either national or liaison leaders in the mid-1960's and that about 60 per cent of both the early and late recruits are active only at the local level. Therefore, the hypothesis can be accepted, those recruited after 1951 tend to compose the lower cadres of the party.[13]

TABLE 2

RELATIONSHIP BETWEEN PERIOD OF RECRUITMENT
AND 1966 RANK IN PARTY

	National (per cent)	Liaison (per cent)	Local (per cent)	Total (per cent)	(n)
Founders	37.5	37.5	25.0	100.0	(16)
Early recruits	15.4	25.0	59.6	100.0	(52)
Late recruits	14.3	28.6	57.1	100.0	(35)
$t_b = 0.156$		$S/\sigma_s = z = 1.73$		$P(1-t) > 0.05$	

The second hypothesis, *that newer recruits were derived from among the lower status social elements of the Costa Rican population,* was tested by constructing a special typology based on age, education, and occupation. Table 3 indicates the percentages in each of the various age brackets. It can readily be seen that most are relatively young since almost 85 per cent of the total fall between twenty-five and fifty-five years. According to these data very old persons do not appear to dominate party positions. This is not surprising, however, since the PLN originated only two decades ago as a youth protest movement. The youthfulness of the leadership cadre is even more pronounced when national leaders are considered separately. Table 4 demonstrates that all national leaders in the sample were less than fifty-five years of age.

The second variable entered into the sociological typology involved an assessment of the educational achievement of the 103 leaders. Table 5 demonstrates that nearly all those inter-

---

include provincial leaders, leaders of important cantons in the hinterland who spent considerable periods of time in the capital, and national party or governmental leaders who were clearly identified with a particular geographic region.

13. All tables were tested for statistical significance at the 0.05 level of probability. This means that all relationships described as "significant" had no more than five chances in a hundred to come about randomly.

TABLE 3

AGE DISTRIBUTION

Age	Per Cent
Under 25	6.8
25–35	23.3
36–45	28.2
46–55	33.0
56–65	7.8
Over 66	1.0
Total	100.1
(n)	(103)

TABLE 4

AGE OF NATIONAL LEADERS

Age	Per Cent
Under 25	21.1
25–45	47.3
46–55	31.6
Over 56	0.0
Total	100.0
(n)	(19)

viewed had high school or university training or their equivalents. In fact, of those claiming university education, 15.8 per cent had studied abroad, which carries more prestige than a local degree. Almost all (80.6 per cent) claimed to have graduated from the highest school they attended or were in the process of finishing when interviewed. The PLN can indeed boast that its leaders are well prepared for their careers.

TABLE 5

EDUCATIONAL ATTAINMENT

Level	Per Cent
Primary school only	11.7
Trade or special school	2.9
High school	24.3
Normal school	5.8
University	55.3
Total	100.0
(n)	(103)

The educational level of the group also manifests itself in the third variable, occupational status. Table 6 compares current occupations with those held at the time of entering the party and the occupations of the group's fathers. Since the study of law is a natural steppingstone to a political career in Latin American nations, it is not surprising that the distribution is heavily weighted in favor of the law profession. It is significant that persons in prestige occupations (professionals, businessmen, and large landowners) provide about half of the total. Few lower class occupations appeared, even among the strictly local leaders. In order to make the totals more workable, university professors, lawyers, physicians, businessmen, large ranchers, university students, and "other professionals" were combined into a single category labeled "professional and business." Schoolteachers, small merchants, white-collar workers, and public employees were collapsed into a "lower-middle-class"

TABLE 6

OCCUPATION

	Current (per cent)	At Time of Entering Party (per cent)	Father's (per cent)
University professor	4.9	1.0	0.0
Lawyer	16.5	8.7	5.0
Physician	4.9	2.9	8.0
Other professionals	9.7	4.9	12.0
Businessmen	7.8	2.9	4.0
Rancher or landowner	4.9	5.8	9.0
Merchant	3.9	2.9	15.0
Schoolteacher	5.8	3.9	2.0
Office worker	8.7	14.6	7.0
Public employee	6.8	1.0	7.0
Urban blue-collar worker	1.9	1.9	7.0
Small farmer	0.0	0.0	16.0
Artisan	3.9	2.9	2.0
Domestic servant	4.9	4.9	5.0
Student	7.8	35.0	0.0
Housewife	5.8	3.9	0.0
Other	1.9	2.9	1.0
Total	100.1	100.1	100.0
(n)	(103)	(103)	(100)*

*Fathers of three of the respondents either died at an early age or were not responsible for their upbringing.

type, and urban blue-collar workers, small farmers, service people, and artisans were labeled "workers." Housewives and "others" were excluded.

The six classifications of age were tabulated against three collapsed classifications of education (university, secondary, primary), and the three collapsed classifications of occupation, yielding a matrix of fifty-six property spaces. Since many of the property spaces were vacant and the leaders tended to cluster, four distinct types emerged and 89 of the 103 could be put in one of the four. "Young intellectuals" are the leaders under thirty-five years of age with university training and either professional and business or lower-white-collar occupations. The "middle-aged intellectuals" are those between thirty-five and sixty-five with university education and either professional and business or lower-middle-class occupations. Leaders with secondary school education and either professional and business or lower-middle-class occupations plus primary-school-educated

TABLE 7

RELATIONSHIP BETWEEN PERIOD OF RECRUITMENT
AND SOCIOLOGICAL TYPE

	Middle-Aged Intellectuals (per cent)	White-Collarites and Proletarians (per cent)	Total	(n)
Founders	85.7	14.3	100.0	(14)
Early recruits	48.8	51.2	100.0	(43)
Late recruits	50.0	50.0	100.0	(10)
	$x^2 = 6.18$	$df = 2$	$P > 0.05$	

leaders with professional and business occupations were labeled "white-collarites"; workers with secondary or primary education plus lower-middle-class types with primary education were classified as "proletarians."

Table 7 illustrates that a significant relationship between period of recruitment and sociological type does exist and the hypothesis can be accepted. Practically all founders were middle-aged intellectuals, while early and late recruits were divided equally between the collapsed types. "Young intellectuals" were eliminated for the obvious reason that most would have been too youn to be a founder or original recruit.

An index of mo! lity was constructed to test the hypothesis *that those who joi d the party after it was founded are more socially mobile* by ulating current occupation of the leaders against occupation of their fathers. The results of that cross-tabulation demonstrate that upward mobility is a characteristic of the leaders in general, for only four individuals proved to be downward mobile (see Table 8). Therefore, only two classifications could be used, "upward mobiles" and "statics," with the few downward mobiles collapsed into the second category.

TABLE 8

SOCIAL MOBILITY

Current Occupation of Leaders*	Occupation of Father* (per cent)		
	Professional & Business (per cent)	Lower-Middle Class (per cent)	Working Class (per cent)
Professional & business	92.6	78.6	20.7
Lower-middle & working class	7.4	21.4	79.3
Total	100.0	100.0	100.0
(n)	(27)	(28)	(29)
$x^2 = 60.97$ $df = 2$ $P > 0.001$			

*Minus students, housewives, and "others."

When tabulated against the independent variable a significant relationship did not exist and the hypothesis was rejected.

A fourth hypothesis, *that later joiners were less political than early joiners*, was tested by asking all leaders the question: "Before beginning activities in the affairs of the party, would you say Costa Rican politics: (1) interested you a great deal, (2) interested you moderately, or (3) did not interest you very much?" Almost two-thirds (62.1 per cent) stated that they had been very interested in politics prior to formal party membership. Another 25.2 per cent stated that they had been moderately interested, and only 12.6 per cent confessed they took little or no interest before their experience with the PLN. A very significant relation does exist between the two variables as Table 9 demonstrates, so the fourth hypothesis can be accepted as valid.

TABLE 9

RELATIONSHIP BETWEEN PERIOD OF RECRUITMENT AND INTEREST IN POLITICS BEFORE JOINING PARTY

	Very Interested (per cent)	Mod. Interested & Not Interested (per cent)	Total (per cent)	(n)
Founders	100.0	0.0	100.0	(16)
Early recruits	61.5	38.5	100.0	(52)
Late recruits	45.7	54.3	100.0	(35)
$x^2 = 13.80$ $df = 2$ $P > 0.01$				

The fifth hypothesis, *that later joiners tend to be more religious,* was tested by asking the leaders to rate themselves according to the intensity of their religious beliefs. This variable proved to be about as important as might be expected in a secular party. Although 90.3 per cent gave their religion as Roman Catholic,[14] only 28.2 per cent considered themselves "very religious." Another 37.9 per cent said they were "moderately religious," and 25.2 per cent described themselves as "not too religious." Finally, 8.7 per cent admitted they were "not religious at all." Estimates of church attendance per month tended to verify the self-appraisals. Only 8.9 per cent of those who answered the question claimed to go to church more than four times per month; 35.6 per cent went less than once per month. A full 34.7 per cent never go to church at all. Regardless of overall attitudes concerning religion, no relationship appeared between the two variables and the hypothesis was rejected.

Authoritarianism is presumably a characteristic of more traditional political systems and also of more traditional outlook. Consequently, if leaders brought into the party after 1951 are more traditionally oriented than the founders, it can be hypothesized *that the later the leader joined the party, the more authoritarian his attitude.* This concept was operationalized by the use of Lane's Authoritarian-Equalitarian (AE) scale. Although the AE scale is an extremely shortened version of the original Adorno "F" scale which included some 585 questionnaire items, it purports to measure some of the latter's major dimensions.[15] One advantage of Lane's method is that it can be scaled according to Guttman's rank order scaling technique.[16] Another advantage is inherent in its brevity and simplicity.

A chief criticism of authoritarian scales concerns "culture boundness." Those who argue against transferring such schedules across national frontiers maintain that measurements devised to study the attitudes of inhabitants of one nation might measure something quite different in another social and political

14. Protestants, 5.8 per cent; Jewish, 1.9 per cent; and no religion, 1.9 per cent.

15. Methodological justification for the AE scale is presented in Robert E. Lane's "Political Personality and Electoral Choice," *American Political Science Review,* pp. 173–90.

16. L. Guttman, "The Basis for Scalogram Analysis," in Samuel Stouffer, et al., *Measurement and Prediction: Studies in Social Psychology in World War II.*

climate with different traditions, customs, values, and outlooks. For this reason the conclusions are presented with caution. However, use of the scale in this case is supported by two factors. First, the high coefficient of reproducibility of the study (0.911) would tend to support the hypothesis that the four questions fall into some sort of single dimensional axis when considered together. Second, Costa Rica, with its tradition of democracy, civil authority, and respect for individual rights is not too different from the United States, where the test was devised. Although the former might be Hispanic in origin, its cultural patterns, political thought, and popular attitudes have been heavily influenced by the United States for over a century.

The questions asked were nearly direct Spanish translations of Lane's items and were distributed as follows:

(1) A few strong leaders could make this country better than all the laws and studies that are made (agree, 68.0 per cent; disagree, 32.0 per cent; no answer, 0.0 per cent).

(2) Many persons say that young people should be more strictly disciplined by their parents (agree, 62.1 per cent; disagree, 36.8 per cent; no answer, 1.0 per cent).

(3) Today there is opportunity for everyone and those who don't get ahead don't have ambition (agree, 55.3 per cent; disagree, 44.7 per cent; no answer, 0.0 per cent).

(4) Many people say that an insult to personal honor or to honor of the family should not be forgotten (agree, 24.3 per cent; disagree, 75.7 per cent; no answer, 0.0 per cent).

The 103 leaders divided into the five possible types on the AE scale according to Table 10. In cases involving doubt due to respondent error the "most numerous category" rule was applied.

It apparently makes no difference whether a person joined the party early or late because both types behave almost identically. Therefore, the hypothesis must be rejected.

The seventh hypothesis under consideration in this series is concerned with the relative ideological outlook of the 103 leaders. Again, ideological content is characteristic of the modernizing party, so it can be hypothesized *that the founders are more ideologically oriented than those they later recruited.* Thirteen open-ended items were inserted into the interview

TABLE 10

POSITION ON AE SCALE

Type	Number	Percentage of Total
I (Most authoritarian)	16	15.5
II	32	31.1
III	18	17.5
IV	13	12.6
V	24	23.3
Total	103	100.0

schedule to aid in distinguishing those persons active in the National Liberation Party — and Costa Rican politics in general — for ideological reasons from those whose overriding political concern centered around nonideological goals such as personal prestige, power, winning elections, building the party machinery, and so forth.[17] It was possible to establish ten types based on the total number of ideological responses offered, and Table 11 lists the distribution of these types. It should not be inferred that those classified as ideologues have no interest in building the

TABLE 11

IDEOLOGICAL RESPONSES

Type	Number of Ideological Responses	Distribution	Percentage of Total
X	0	1	1.0
IX	1	8	7.8
VIII	2	18	17.5
VII	3	20	19.4
VI	4	15	14.6
V	5	9	8.7
IV	6	14	13.6
III	7	13	12.6
II	8	3	2.9
I	9	2	1.9
Total		103	100.0

17. For example, one of the thirteen items asked: "Do you really believe there are genuine differences between the PLN and other Costa Rican political parties?" Both ideological and power-oriented answers were given by different respondents: "We are the only party really trying to help the poor people better themselves," and "Liberación is the only Costa Rican party organized on a permanent basis with committees in all parts of the Republic." The other twelve questions yielded similar response patterns.

party and winning elections, or power activists are devoid of principle and philosophy. However, it is true that members of the former group think (and presumably behave) in ideological terms, whereas members of the second group are motivated by power goals.

Although later joiners tended to be less ideological than early joiners, the relationship did not prove significant and this hypothesis was also rejected.

The final hypothesis attempts to differentiate the types of leaders according to their view of the relative "openness" of the National Liberation Party. All 103 interviewees were asked: "Some persons believe that only a few leaders of the party, or only a few closed groups, make the majority of decisions in the party and also decide who will be its leaders in the future. Do you believe this is so? Why?" If any real difference exists between the founders and those they recruited regarding outlook and concepts of authority, the originals could be expected to view the party as more open and not run by closed groups. However, this did not prove to be so. Absolutely no relation was found and the proposition was rejected.

General Conclusions

Chapters 2, 3, and 4 concern the first of LaPalombara and Weiner's criteria, that the modern party must be continuous *and able to survive the political careers of any particular leaders or group of leaders.* Since the National Liberation Party has not been in existence more than a generation as this is written, the hypothesis that the PLN is continuous (as defined) can only be accepted tenuously at best. Moreover, a series of splits and internal conflicts during the past few years have seriously threatened the future of the party. As this is written immediately prior to the 1970 election, it cannot be stated with certainty whether the PLN will be able to survive the present crisis or whether it will disintegrate in the decade ahead. If Figueres is successful—which is highly probable, only because the opposition is *even more fragmented* than the PLN—the prestige of office and patronage power will undoubtedly give the beleaguered party new life, at least temporarily. Yet, it seems reasonable to assume that come the worst the PLN will continue as a political structure in Costa Rican politics, perhaps weakened and only a shadow of its once-powerful self but a recognizable entity nonetheless. Therefore, the hypothesis that the party is continuous will be *cautiously and tentatively accepted.* At the present time there is no definite reason to believe that the leaders recruited after 1951 will not carry on (in one fashion or another) after the founders retire.

In terms of outlook and attitudes, those recruited since 1951 do not appear greatly different from the original founders. Although they do tend to come from the less privileged social sectors and are less educated, their *weltanschauungen* seems more or less the same. They are not significantly more authoritarian or less ideological. They did tend to admit being less interested in national politics at the time of recruitment, but this is probably a function of lesser previous opportunity to actively engage in the political life of the nation.

5. National Liberation Party Structural Interaction

T HIS CHAPTER measures the National Liberation Party against LaPalombara and Weiner's second criterion, that the modern political party must be permanently organized at the local levels and that local leaders must regularly communicate and otherwise interact with the national leaders. First, an overview of the formal structure of the party is presented in order to acquaint the reader with the way the PLN is run, then data concerning the permanence of local units are presented. Third, the nature of national-local leadership differences is taken up, and finally a series of hypotheses pertaining to the factional rivalries and their effect on local units is presented and tested.

An Overview of the Formal Structure

Although the new party had not yet become fully operational, especially at the district or barrio level, in time for the 1953 election, Figueres' easy victory insured continued popular enthusiasm. During the next four years the structure was improved, and in 1958 a completely organized party was put into action. Since 1958 the internal structure of the party has remained essentially the same. National Liberation's basic unit of organization in urban areas is the barrio (neighborhood) executive committee which is composed of five persons. The barrio committee appoints all *jefes de manzana* (block captains) and supervises registration of party members and voter turnout. Although voter transportation is sometimes channeled through the barrio committee in highly urban areas, this important function is usually left to higher authority. In very rural areas barrio organization is unknown and district committees form the lowest party units.

Barrio committees are theoretically elected by assemblies composed of all local registered voters who had previously "adhered" to the party, but in practice they are often appointed by cantonal officers. These assemblies, when actually held, are strictly partisan affairs conducted entirely under the auspices of local party functionaries. The North American practice of electing party officers at public polls is entirely unknown in Costa Rica. All members of all barrio executive committees within a given district compose the district assembly which elects a five-man district executive committee. Again, in actual practice many district committees are appointed from the top as well.

The district executive committee supposedly meets once per month and is officially charged with "promoting interests of the party, fighting for the well-being of the district, executing the instructions of higher party organs, and serving as a liaison between the bulk of PLN voters and the party."[1] In urban areas these committees often comprise a no-man's land between highly effective barrio committees and the more important cantonal committees. Much direct contact exists between the latter two, so district leaders are bypassed. District committees function best in semirural areas where one small town serves as a center of district activity and committee members are clustered in or close to that center. A phenomenon characteristic of district organization in the more rural areas is caciquismo or bossism. Often a particular merchant or rancher will enjoy considerable patronage from local campesinos and will use his influence to control local party organs.

At the cantonal level the executive committee becomes a

1. Partido Liberación Nacional, Estatutos (May 1965), Article 19. Actually, district committees seldom meet in noncampaign years.

genuine decision-making body. With two exceptions – the capital of San José, where the various cantons have been combined to form a large metropolitan area, and the previously mentioned small rural towns which serve as centers of districts – cantonal committees provide the only effective link between the national party and the electorate. Local clubs, run by cantonal committees, serve as meeting places during electoral campaigns where neighbors can meet on an informal basis, obtain PLN literature, fraternize, and discuss current politics. Cantonal assemblies, again composed of all members of all district executive committees, theoretically elect ten committeemen who subsequently choose a president, secretary, and treasurer from among their own number; in practice, these officers are often appointed by the current presidential candidate or his lieutenants. Caciquismo is also apparent in rural areas at this level, but is not as prominent as at lower levels. National statutes insist that at least five of the ten committee members must permanently reside in the central district of their respective canton,[2] but in fact, almost all cantonal committeemen reside in the cantonal capitals. Since a large percentage of Costa Rican voters live within the geographical boundaries of the central districts in each canton, this means that district committees in central districts are at best duplications of their respective cantonal committees and are therefore rendered relatively useless. Most of the party faithful have contact only with cantonal officials.

Although party statutes provide for provincial executive committees at the next superior level,[3] only three provinces have ever attempted instituting such organizations. In Heredia and Cartago such committees function very weakly, and in Guanacaste a paper organization exists. Provincial assemblies, composed of five delegates from each canton theoretically chosen by cantonal assemblies, are also weak and serve only two effective functions – selecting ten delegates to serve on the National Party Assembly[4] and recommending candidates for the Costa Rican Legislative Assembly.

At the national level, the Party Assembly is the chief legislative-like organ since the National PLN Congress is only a decentra-

2. Ibid., Article 23.   3. Ibid., Articles 26, 27, and 28.

4. To avoid confusion between the PLN National Assembly and the Costa Rican Legislative Assembly, the former will be referred to as the Party Assembly and the latter as the Legislative Assembly or the legislature.

lized poll for selecting presidential candidates.[5] It is composed of ten delegates from each province, meets once every two years, and is coordinated by the national secretary of organization, who serves as a member of both the National Executive Directory and the National Secretariat-General. It selects the three members of the National Executive Committee, secretaries, members of the Disciplinary Committee, all candidates for the Costa Rican Legislative Assembly (upon advice from the seven provincial assemblies), and ratifies the party's candidates for president of the Republic and local municipal offices. In addition to these duties, the Party Assembly is responsible for introducing modifications and changes in the party's rules and generally supervising its management. Although Article 31 of the national statutes also charges it with carrying out the acts of the National PLN Congress, the ineffectiveness of the latter negates action of this sort. Criticism of the Party Assembly has centered around the allegations that it meets too infrequently to provide effective overall leadership and that it is "highly influenced" by the persons or groups that dominate the Directory.

The National Executive Directory, usually called simply the Directory, operates the day-to-day business of the party and is a genuine center of power. It is composed of all ten national secretaries, the three members of the National Executive Committee, plus the chief of the Parliamentary Fraction. Actually the Directory is usually considerably larger since subsecretaries of certain secretariats, the chairman of the Disciplinary Committee, and four additional deputies are often seated. Leadership of the group is entrusted to the National Executive Committee consisting of the party's president (usually Figueres), secretary general, and treasurer. They are "elected" by the Party Assembly (which they control) to two-year terms and may be re-elected. All three may represent the party legally and are ultimately responsible for the conduct of party activities. They are not obliged to meet regularly but usually do so during campaign periods.

The National Secretariat-General fulfills the line functions of the party. All ten secretaries (Organization, Plans, Youth Affairs, Feminine Affairs, Municipal Affairs, Finance, Foreign Affairs,

5. The National PLN Congress is considered in detail on pages 77–78.

Publicity, Propaganda, and Doctrine and Leadership) are elected by the Party Assembly for two-year terms. In one case, Youth Affairs, the secretary general of Juventud Liberactionista serves as national secretary as well. Subsecretaries are elected directly by the Directory, upon recommendation of the secretary in question. During political campaigns the secretariats require nearly full-time attendance and six of the ten secretaries receive monetary compensation averaging about $500 (U.S.) monthly (1966).

Auxiliary Organizations

Three major lateral organizations are maintained by the National Liberation Party—Juventud Liberacionista, a women's section, and an armed security corps. In addition, a number of loosely affiliated sports and recreational clubs usually pop up around election time, and Rerum Novarum, a former labor federation, was virtually part of the party until the mid-1960's. The clubs are too irregular to merit further comment, and the Liberationist labor movement is considered in chapter 8.

The youth movement, Juventud Liberacionista (JL), was, at the height of its power in 1966, the largest auxiliary group by far, claiming 40,000 members in 250 local committees. The JL traces its heritage directly to the Center for the Study of National Problems and considers Eloy Morua, a youth active in the Social Democratic Party, its founder. Although Morua was killed in military action in 1949, long before the Juventud was established, his partisan publications during the 1945–49 period are rich with suggestions and plans to motivate the nation's youth. Morua's activities had set the pace and in 1952, three years after his death, a Youth Committee was formed to aid the candidacy of José Figueres. That committee, led by Rodrigo Carazo, Armando Arauz, José Rafael Cordero, and Rodolfo Solano, remained small and functioned only in San José, but the nucleus for a larger organization was established. In 1957 the activities of the committee were expanded; twenty-one local committees were founded in all provincial capitals and principal cantons but all acted independently and were not coordinated on a national scale. Most local committees functioned so well, however, that a national youth auxiliary was created shortly after the 1958 election and the present name, Juventud Liberacionista, was adopted. Chiefly responsible for the creation of the new organization were two San José youths, Jaime Darenblum and Alfonso Lara.

Within a year the new group split over the question of Fidel Castro. The leadership, especially Darenblum and Lara, took the position that Castro had strong Communist leanings and would soon pose a threat to hemispheric peace and solidarity. They adopted, in the name of the entire organization, a resolution denouncing the Cuban dictator and his growing (at that time) influence in Costa Rica. The JL's left wing, many of whose members were affiliated with a contemporary pro-Castro group called the Society of Friends of the Cuban Revolution, was strongly organized, and in 1959 its leaders, Fernando Salazar, Alexis Gomez, and Fermin Alvarado, succeeded in ousting Darenblum and Lara. Salazar was elected secretary general, a post he occupied until 1964.[6]

The First National JL Congress was held in 1960. A set of ideological propositions was adopted and its internal structure was reorganized somewhat in order to parallel the regular party. A National Directory, varying between fifteen and twenty members, manages the business of the entire organization and coordinates four "occupational-situational" sectors, each of which theoretically maintains separate local committees. The Student Sector is the most active and is divided into two sub-sectors, one for high schools, the other for the University of Costa Rica. A Rural Sector and a Metropolitan Sector, which includes the city of San José and environs, duplicate the Student Sector. The fourth, the Workers Sector, originally instituted to organize young industrial workers into committees based on a single factory or plant, has been a paper organization. Much of the difficulty arises from the fact that Costa Rica, an agricultural nation, has very little industry and few plants large enough to support an active committee.

Between 1960 and 1968 JL grew steadily, came to occupy a position of considerable strength within the regular party, and at the apex of its influence suddenly collapsed. A series of capable general secretaries (Jaime Darenblum, 1958–59; Fernando Salazar, 1959–64; and Oscar Soley, 1964–68) gave the JL a strong voice on the National Directory. The candidacy of Daniel Oduber in 1966 contributed greatly to the group's stature and

6. The organization became disenchanted with Castro soon thereafter and in 1961 denounced his methods.

importance because Oduber, on the outs with conservative elements in the party, had to rely very heavily on the left-leaning Juventud. The youths, in turn, adopted Oduber as a hero and worked long hours on his behalf.

Unfortunately for the JL, Oduber turned his back on the PLN's left wing in 1968 by supporting Figueres' nomination for the 1970 presidential election (see footnote 10, chapter 4). After 1966 the youths increasingly perceived Figueres a conservative influence and a staunch defender of the *status quo*. Previously he had been regarded as the "balancer" of the Party, as the great caudillo ever above internecine conflicts, as Mr. Liberation himself. The PLN left, which includes virtually the whole of the Juventud, cites his huge accumulation of personal wealth, his advanced age, and his insistence on free enterprise economic principles as examples of his conservatism. It is also greatly disturbed by the high-handed way he runs the party. The fact is that youths of the late 1940's and 1950's were no longer particularly young in the late 1960's. A totally new generation had taken over the Juventud, and its outlook was considerably different. Although Figueres had been a brave, dashing, and progressive rebel fighter to their fathers and older brothers, he was considered little more than a stodgy old has-been by members of National Liberation's "now generation."

As a result, the Juventud has consistently taken an anti-establishment position in recent years. It tended to side with Rodrigo Carazo in his bitter 1968 nomination battle with Figueres. Carazo, formerly Figueres' protégé and, in a sense, a founder of the JL, was not really considered a youth hero, hence the support was merely anti-Figueres in nature. Second, it urged Alfonso Carro to seek the nomination, and passed, by a large majority, a declaration urging him to run at its Second National Congress in 1968. Third, and most important, Juventud leaders collaborated with older leftists to frame the Declaration of the Patio de Agua described elsewhere. The youth enthusiastically supported the Patio de Agua principles and attempted, with no success, to incorporate them into the regular party program. Officially, a diminished Juventud Liberacionista reluctantly supported Figueres and the regular PLN during the 1970 campaign. Manuel Carballo, an energetic and competent leftist lawyer in his late twenties, emerged as leader of the JL faction that favored supporting the party candidate regardless of preferences or convictions; he subsequently became JL secretary general in 1968. The Juventud is presently a shadow of its former self and is eager to overthrow the older leadership or bolt the PLN altogether.

The Women's Section of the PLN has not been so controversial. Because José Figueres had insisted that women be integrated into party councils on an equal basis, no separate women's auxiliary was created in conjunction with the 1953 election. Francisco Orlich, however, believed such an organization could be useful and in 1957 the Directory hastily created committees in about two-thirds of the nation's cantons. A general lack of efficiency quickly convinced the party leaders to subdue such activity, so the committees were allowed to fade out after the 1958 election. It was not until 1964 that the present organization was reinstituted. Cecilia Gonzales de Penrod began organizing, of her own volition and without express authority, a national Women's Section with local committees at the cantonal level. Her work met with initial success, so she subsequently petitioned the 1964 Party Assembly to create a new Secretariat of Feminine Affairs to supervise the Section she had created. About thirty-five local committees with a claimed total membership of 2,500 were established in conjunction with both the 1966 and 1970 campaigns. Since the women's organization closely parallels the regular party (in which women participate), the overall effectiveness of the group has been questioned. Yet, it has provided valuable assistance such as sewing green and white party flags, providing door-to-door canvassers, and driving voters to the polls.

Unlike the youth and feminine auxiliaries, the paramilitary security corps of the party is, at best, an "extralegal" organization that functions in a secretive manner without publicity. Currently called the Security Committee, this group is a lineal descendant of the Army of National Liberation which successfully waged the 1948 civil war. After the war, troops were maintained on a standby basis, and in the early 1950's Figueres' government reinstituted his private Army of National Liberation as the Reserva Nacional, an agency of the Costa Rican government. Hence it became a partisan organization acting as an official public military force. In 1955 supporters of ex-President Calderón Guardia launched an attack from Nicaragua but were repelled by the Liberationist National Reserve forces. Again placed on standby after 1955, the security corps diminished in size until it was reorganized for the 1962 election. It was felt that Calderón, running as a presidential candidate, might attempt a coup, so about 5,000 armed veterans gathered into local committees which were commanded nationally by Frank Marshall Jimenez. Between 1962 and 1966 the active Security Committee numbered less than a thousand, although a much larger force of militarily trained party members could be quickly organized in case of emergency.[7] Members are organized into local groups about the size of army squads. During campaign periods they drill one Sunday per month and from time to time receive training films and demonstrations on the use of weapons. They also serve as bodyguards for the party's candidate and police meetings and rallies. An around-the-clock alert was called for a three-day period at the time of the 1966 election, and security people were obligated to remain tuned to the party's radio station for coded instructions in case of emergency. Although the station was ostensibly used to coordinate voter transportation units, the highly mobile Security Committee could have been quickly activated by broadcasting coded directions.

The Parliamentary Fraction

All PLN members elected to the Legislative Assembly compose the Parliamentary Fraction which is, in contrast to the "Congressional Party" in the United States, an integrated and formal organ of the party hierarchy. Legislators are responsible to both the National Directory and the National Party Assembly and are subject to discipline. In return, the fraction has five seats on the Directory; its chief is an *ex officio* member and four others are elected by caucus. Deputies are also expected to contribute financially to the party. A fixed 10 per cent of their salaries goes to the national PLN treasury,[8] but a portion of it is returned to the fraction's officers to defray office expenses.

The Parliamentary Fraction is free to establish its own operat-

7. Due to the secretive nature of the Security Committee, the author cannot supply accurate detailed information as to current size and proficiency. Party leaders, most of whom refused comment altogether, were reluctant to disclose facts which might jeopardize the party's position.

8. Deputies are paid $18.75 (U.S.) per session in the Legislative Assembly; party contributions average about $50 per month. In addition, legislators are expected to help pay off the party's campaign debts and are assessed extra amounts (about $3,000 per deputy in 1966) following elections.

ing rules and elect its own officers. Although it is in no way bound to adopt the rules of its predecessors,[9] past fractions have changed or modified earlier procedures only slightly. The caucus, which meets weekly, elects a chief, vice chief, secretary, treasurer, and coordinator,[10] who jointly compose the Directory of the Parliamentary Fraction. Although voting discipline is required on "political questions," the Directory has no effective means of forcing wayward legislators to support the party line. Current regulations give the fraction chief the right to impose a $3.75 (U.S.) fine, but this practice is seldom followed; patronage power is not important due to Costa Rica's multimember district system and constitutional prohibitions on re-election. As a result, the Jefe de Fracción has little of the power or influence possessed by floor leaders of the United States Congress. In the words of Fernando Volio, National Liberation's 1966–67 fraction chief, "the Chief has to be considered a good leader. If other deputies trust him and respect him they will maintain party discipline and support the Fraction Directory, if not, each will vote as he chooses."[11]

Strict discipline can be maintained on extremely important bills, however, by a device known as the united party vote. The Fraction Directory or any PLN deputy may request that such a vote be taken in caucus, and if a two-thirds majority agree that party discipline must be maintained, all deputies are obliged to vote in a bloc. A breach of the rules at this point must be reported to the PLN's National Disciplinary Committee. Only twice in the legislative history of the National Liberation Party have deputies broken discipline following a united party vote.

Party Finance

The national secretary of finance is the party's collection manager and is ultimately responsible for gathering all monthly contributions in the entire nation. Although the PLN does not collect regular dues from its members as many European parties do, activists are expected to pledge monthly "voluntary gifts" which range from five colones ($.75 U.S.) to 150 colones ($22.50

9. Because the Costa Rican Constitution does not permit re-election of deputies, an entirely new set of lawmakers is present each legislative term.
10. The coordinator fulfills the same function as the Whip in the United States legislative system.
11. Interview (May 26, 1966).

U.S.) in a few rare cases. About 70 per cent of all contributions, however, range from $3.25 to $7.50 and the average is about $5.00. These amounts must be collected month after month by the finance secretary, his two paid assistants, and several dozen part-time volunteers. The usual method of collection involves appointing a single person in each large private company, shop, or governmental agency and making him responsible in his place of employment only; practically no attempt is made to collect monthly gifts from rural persons. The party spends this income directly and no capital is invested in stocks or securities, with the rare exception of short-term bank bonds.

Electoral campaigns are partially financed by the government. Law provides that 2 per cent of a single year's national budget[12] be divided among all parties receiving more than 10 per cent of the total vote.[13] Payments are made within three or four months to all eligible parties in the form of government bonds paying interest and redeemable four years from date of issue. Provisions have been made by the Costa Rican Legislative Assembly, however, to allow the nationally owned banks to purchase the bonds at full face value. Therefore, campaign debts can be paid relatively soon after each election.

The major financial problem faced by the PLN has been in acquiring sufficient operating funds during the campaign, months before government subsidies can be received. Two methods have been employed. First, nonreturnable "free campaign gifts" are solicited from the more affluent party members. Second, reimbursable loans of up to $1,500 (U.S.) are obtained from other affluent supporters and are repaid from the government subsidies after the election. Since National Liberation's share of the governmental grant has never equaled the entire amount of loans collected, lending members have never been paid back in full. In addition, it is customary to retain the first 20 to 30 per cent of the governmental reimbursements for postelectoral debts and current operating costs, which also

12. The average yearly budget for the immediate three-year period preceding each election is used for purposes of calculating total campaign expenditures.

13. The votes received by each party for all three electoral contests (president, deputies, and municipal officers) are added together and used as a numerator in calculating its share of the total grant. In 1966 only two of the five parties entering candidates in the February election received governmental funds because of the 10 per cent rule.

lowers the total capital available for repaying the loans. As a result, the wealthy persons in the PLN, as in most Western parties, retain economic power in decision-making circles that is disproportionate to their numbers. Since most affluent members are associated with the party's conservative wing, leftist elements convincingly argue that the system is weighted in favor of the right.

The Nomination Process

Since only three types of public officials (local municipal council members, deputies to the single-chambered Legislative Assembly, and the president plus two vice-presidents) are elected, all at the same time, the electoral process is very simple. Voters are obligated to go to the polls only once every four years and choose lists of candidates from three very short ballots. Therefore, nominating public officials is uncomplicated. Municipal officers are theoretically nominated by cantonal party assemblies from a list of local party members having previously expressed interest in the position. Although the National Party Assembly must technically ratify all such nominations, it has interferred little in such local matters. Only cases involving party members previously punished by the Discipline Committee merit national attention. One recognized flaw in the system involves caciquismo. Since some cantonal organizations are controlled by bosses, official PLN candidates for local offices are often the handpicked friends of a single person or a small clique. The party has made several attempts to democratize local intraparty elections, but old traditions have proven difficult to change.

Candidates for the Costa Rican Legislative Assembly are chosen in a similar manner, although the National Party Assembly (i.e., the Directory which controls it) takes a more active role. Provincial assemblies suggest the names of three to twenty-one candidates (depending on size of provinces) to the National Party Assembly for its consideration. Since provincial party assemblies are weak, the National Party Assembly has taken the position that it must directly oversee all candidates for national office. Usually a well-known leader in the province will nominate the candidate for the first several positions,[14] and it is understood

14. Under Costa Rica's system of proportional representation, the candidate occupying first position in a given province is almost certain of election; a name placed further down the list will have progressively slimmer chances of victory.

that those nominees are the "official" choices. Although the legislative candidates, as well as the positions they are to occupy on their respective provincial lists, are determined by national and provincial leaders beforehand, any delegate may propose an alternate: on rare occasions the "official" candidates have been defeated or placed lower down on the list.

After 1958 the PLN employed a system of selecting presidential candidates that combined the convention system and primaries. Previously, huge conventions (National Congresses) were held in San José every four years about eight months before elections. Because such conventions required transporting between 3,000 and 4,000 delegates from all parts of the nation, the cost became prohibitive. Consequently, the PLN National Assembly changed the method in 1961; convocation is no longer required. Although the name "National Congress" remained, delegates simply vote at local party polling places within their respective cantons. Requirements for voting are very broad because the party has attempted to include all active members and militants. Those eligible are: members of all barrio, district, cantonal, provincial, and national committees; any regular party member who has ever held an elective or appointive governmental position; any regular party member who has ever served on the board of directors of any governmental autonomous institution; and all regular members who have ever served as officers of certain loosely affiliated trade unions, cooperatives, and sports clubs.[15]

Although the above arrangement appears as open and democratic as any yet devised, it has come under increasing attack in recent years, particularly from the PLN's left wing. Apparently, minor or peripheral party leaders play little or no role in selecting the presidential candidate, and the decision is left to higher-ups: leaders not usually lower than about the cantonal level, that is, partisan activists ranking with American county chairmen or above. Hence, whoever controls the party machinery controls the nomination process as well; since Figueres (and the most recent PLN presidental candidate, who has either been Figueres himself or a close political ally) has always dominated the machinery, he has been able to name past candidates personally. As long as Figueres retained his image as Great Mediator, the question of manipulation was largely academic. National Libera-

15. To appear on the intraparty nominating ballot, a petition of 200 signatures is required.

tion Party leaders seemed to prefer a "decision from above" to open and exhausting factional fights. The leftists may not have welcomed the candidacy of Orlich in 1958 or 1962 and the conservatives may have balked at Oduber in 1966, but the majority accepted don Pepe's choices. In recent years, however, Figueres managed to lose his "balancer" position in the party by becoming identified with conservative elements. As a result, he has been severely criticized for "rigging" his own nomination in 1968. Leftist leaders insist that the alliance of Figueres and Oduber (who has since been disowned by many of his former leftist supporters) was enough to railroad the nomination for the Hero of 1948.

According to Costa Rica's Electoral Code, the presidential candidate must be technically elected by the National Party Assembly. In order to fulfill this requirement, the assembly meets about four months after the PLN Congress has chosen the candidate and ratifies the selection. Two vice presidential candidates are also chosen in a manner similar to that employed in the selection of deputies. Names of candidates for all offices are then officially delivered to the Costa Rican Supreme Tribunal of Elections to be certified and placed on their respective ballots.

The above description of the formal organizational structure of the National Liberation Party is concerned with the way things are supposed to be and, to some extent, the way they actually are as judged from the outside. Thus, the first criterion of the hypothesis appears to be met. The PLN is a complex organization which maintains many internal units including national structures; provincial, cantonal, and local structures; auxiliary structures such as the Juventud Liberacionista youth movement and the national Women's Sector; and governmental structures such as the Parliamentary Fraction in the Costa Rican Legislative Assembly, activists in the executive branch, and the PLN members of local municipal councils. The second criterion, that local leaders communicate and interact with national leaders in a regular fashion, will now be considered. The next three sections measure the major dimensions of intraparty relations from the inside, from the viewpoint of the party's local and national leaders.

Local Unit Stability and Vertical Interaction

An item in the interview schedule, "Precisely, what is it you did (you are doing) to win the election of 1966?" was designed to yield information concerning the activity of local leaders. It proved unworkable, however, since all leaders at all levels offered the same responses: they either restated their position in the party ("I'm treasurer of the cantonal committee, I keep the financial records of the party here") or they offered general campaign activities ("I made three speeches," "I put up a number of party flags on buildings"), or both. The item yielded no workable categories, but it did point up the fact that all local leaders were actively engaged in the 1966 campaign (or at least wanted to make the interviewer think they were). No evidence was discovered that local leaders are inactive at such times (although there were indications that some of the leaders, particularly the older ones, had not given their all).

Although the local units of the party are active during electoral campaigns, they do not function in nonelection years. The question, "Does the party sponsor functions such as meetings, rallies, dances, picnics, and so forth in years in which there is no political campaign?"[16] was answered in the affirmative by only 23.6 per cent. Most of those who stated that functions were held in off-election years quickly added that they were of a purely business nature, and no one suggested that social events were sponsored by the party at such times. However, most JL leaders stated that on rare occasions their auxiliary organization organized social affairs for the party's young people.

Another method of getting at the question of local unit continuity involves the tenure of local leaders. If local units are continuous over time, and not simply refounded every four years by the national leaders, sizeable numbers of local leaders should hold their jobs for relatively long periods. Unfortunately, this concept does not take into account either horizontal mobility (remaining active in the party over long periods but changing duties frequently at the same level) or vertical mobility within the local range (for example, movement from the neighborhood or district level to the cantonal level). A separate question in the interview schedule concerning past positions would have allowed this variable to be controlled, but it proved unworkable. In any event, some idea can be obtained about local unit continuity by examining tenure directly. Table 12 lists

16. This question presented several translation problems. The Spanish version read: "Tienen Uds. actividades en el Partido como reuniones, mítines, bailes, paseos, etc. en tiempos que no son de la política?"

the accumulative percentages of the tenure of the fifty-two active local leaders interviewed[17] and proves that 26.9 per cent of the sample held the same position for at least two campaigns. Therefore, *it seems that local units are not completely reorganized at each election.*

TABLE 12

TENURE OF LOCAL LEADERS

Number of Years in Present Position	Accumulative Percentage
More than 12	9.6
11–12	11.5
9–10	17.3
7–8	20.0
5–6	26.9
3–4	61.5
1–2	88.5
Less than 1	100.0
(n)	(52)

TABLE 13

LOCAL LEADERS' CONTACT WITH PROVINCIAL AND NATIONAL LEADERS

Category	Provincial Leaders (per cent)	National Leaders (per cent)
1	27.3	7.3
2	47.3	16.4
3	21.8	40.0
4	3.6	36.4
Total	100.0	100.1
(n)	(55)	(55)

Vertical communication was measured by asking the fifty-five local leaders: "In relation to your work in the party, how often have you had contact with the most important provincial leaders?" The respondents were then asked to choose one of the four categories that best suited their degree of contact. The four categories were: (1) frequently, at least four times per year;

17. Three local leaders were not active at the time of interview.

(2) frequently during political campaigns, but almost never on other occasions; (3) on rare occasions only; (4) almost never.

The question was then repeated changing provincial leaders to national leaders. Table 13 summarizes the results and compares contact with the two levels. It can be seen that those with a local basis of partisan action have far more contact with provincial than with national leaders. Although they frequently meet with their immediate superiors, especially during campaign years, the vast majority seldom come into contact with the party's highest officers.

When local and liaison leaders meet with national leaders they discuss a variety of issues. Table 14 itemizes the answers

TABLE 14

ISSUES DISCUSSED WITH LOCAL AND
LIAISON LEADERS' SUPERIORS

	Per Cent	(n)
PLN organization, strength, and campaign techniques	51.2	43
PLN ideology and program	23.8	20
Respondents' responsibility in the party	21.4	18
Condition of party in respondents' community or auxiliary organization	21.4	18
Current politics and governmental policy	16.7	14
Problems of local community or local persons	14.3	12
Other	3.6	3

to the question: "What type of things do you discuss with your superiors in the party?" Generally, leaders are more prone to discuss "power-oriented" subjects than purely ideological ones, but this is probably due to the tendency of many local leaders to meet with higher officers during campaign periods when party strength is of overriding importance. Multiple responses account for the fact that the totals of Table 14 equal more than 100.0 per cent.

To summarize this section, it seems that: (1) local units are active at elections but not between elections; (2) enough local leaders hold the same jobs from one election to another so local units are not simply new creations every four years; and (3) local leaders do not communicate regularly with national leaders but they do communicate with intermediate leaders, who presumably relay information to and from San José.[18] Therefore, although it seems that the party goes into a four-year hibernation at the local levels, it does remain intact and "reorganizable" for the next electoral battle. If Costa Rica held elections more often, the local units would probably function a great deal more regularly from year to year.

Social and Attitudinal Differences between Leadership Ranks

Having established that local units do operate in a permanent manner, the nature of the differences between the various levels of party leaders will now be analyzed. If the PLN is a modern

TABLE 15

RELATIONSHIP BETWEEN PARTY RANK
AND SOCIOLOGICAL TYPE

	Young & Middle-Aged Intellectuals (per cent)	White-Collarites & Proletarians (per cent)	Total (per cent)	(n)
National	94.4	5.6	100.0	(18)
Liaison	81.5	18.5	100.0	(27)
Local	47.7	52.3	100.0	(44)
	$x^2 = 16.32$	$df = 2$	$P > 0.001$	

and pluralistic political party encouraging mass participation in the lower levels, the hypothesis, *that local leaders are different from national leaders in terms of background and interests*, should hold true. A series of subhypotheses will be presented in order to test this assumption.

The first subhypothesis of the series is *that local leaders stem from lower status social elements than national leaders*. The sociological types described in chapter 4 were tabulated against party rank and the results were found to be statistically significant. Therefore, this hypothesis can be accepted. Table 15 demonstrates a strong relationship between the two variables.

18. Some confusion may arise concerning the differences between provincial and liaison leaders. Although the two types occupy the same relative position in the party hierarchy and are greatly overlapping (many of the twenty-nine liaison leaders were provincial leaders), enough individuals were interviewed who were neither purely national nor purely local, yet maintained no formal connection with their province's party organization, that a separate type had to be created combining all those of intermediate rank in the party.

Since local leaders tend to come from the lower social levels in relation to the national leaders (almost all of whom have already "made it"), it should follow that the local leaders represent the more energetic elements within their levels and are in politics as a means of bettering their social position. Hence, the second hypothesis, *that local leaders are more mobile than national leaders*, should also be expected. Cross-tabulating the

TABLE 16

RELATIONSHIP BETWEEN PARTY RANK AND INTEREST
IN POLITICS BEFORE JOINING PARTY

	Very Interested (per cent)	Interested (per cent)	Not Interested (per cent)	Total (per cent)	(n)
National	94.7	5.3	0.0	100.0	(19)
Liaison	69.0	24.1	6.9	100.0	(29)
Local	47.3	32.7	20.0	100.0	(55)
	$x^2 = 15.19$	$df = 2$	$P > 0.001$		

Two of the nine boxes (22 per cent) in this table had expected frequencies of less than five. Although the author is aware that not more than 20 per cent of all boxes should have an expected frequency less than five, it was decided to accept the slight excess in this case.

mobility types described in chapter 4 with party rank, however, proved that no relation existed, and the second hypothesis had to be rejected.

The third hypothesis also follows from the first. If local leaders come from lower status elements and are therefore deprived of many of the cultural advantages of the first, they could reasonably be expected to be closer to Costa Rican traditions, and therefore somewhat more "traditional." Hence, it should follow *that at the time of entering the party, local leaders were less interested in national politics than were national leaders.* This subhypothesis also proved significant and was accepted. Table 16 tabulates the two variables.

If local leaders are more traditionally oriented *they should be more concerned with religion than are national leaders.* However, this did not prove the case; all three types of leaders behaved in a nearly identical fashion. The hypothesis was rejected.

If more traditionally oriented, local leaders can also be expected to maintain more authoritarian attitudes. Therefore, the fifth hypothesis of this series is *that leaders of the party's*

lower ranks tend to be more authoritarian than their superiors.
The hypothesis proved valid and a strong relation does exist
between the leadership types and positions on the AE scale as
Table 17 demonstrates. Authoritarianism, however, is usually
associated with education, and it is highly probable that national
leaders tend to be less authoritarian because they are better
educated.

TABLE 17

RELATIONSHIP BETWEEN PARTY RANK AND AUTHORITARIANISM

	Authoritarians (AE Types I & II, per cent)	Equalitarians (AE Types III, IV, & V, per cent)	Total (per cent)	(n)
National	21.1	78.9	100.0	(19)
Liaison	27.6	72.4	100.0	(29)
Local	65.5	34.5	100.0	(55)
	$x^2 = 17.05$	$df = 2$	$P > 0.001$	

The sixth hypothesis, *that lower leaders tend to be less ideological than their superiors,* proved to be true as Table 18 demonstrates. About half of the national and liaison leaders fell into the
collapsed type labeled "ideologues," but only three out of ten
local leaders appeared there. Oddly enough, proportionally more
national leaders than liaison leaders fell into the other extreme
("power activists"), although the percentage of local leaders in
the category was greater than either.

The last hypothesis of the series, *that national leaders perceive
the National Liberation Party as more open and democratic than
do local leaders,* should hold true since it has already been
shown that national leaders are more equalitarian and ideological
than local leaders. To test this assumption, a special typology was

TABLE 18

RELATIONSHIP BETWEEN RANK IN THE NATIONAL LIBERATION PARTY
AND IDEOLOGICAL OUTLOOK

	Ideologues (Types I–V per cent)	Moderates (Types VI–VII, per cent)	Power Activists (Types VIII–X, per cent)	Total (per cent)	(n)
National	52.6	21.1	26.3	100.0	(19)
Liaison	48.3	37.9	13.8	100.0	(29)
Local	30.9	36.4	32.7	100.0	(55)
	t_b 0.174	$S/\sigma_s = z = 1.95$	$P > 0.03$		

created based on (1) openness of the party and (2) factionalism. A matrix of four theoretically possible property spaces was obtained and is reproduced in Table 19. Those who believed the PLN has internal factions and is also run by a closed group (either of one faction or both in coalition) were labeled "oligarchs"; those who do not see factions but do see closed groups were labeled "establishmentarians" (after the British usage); "pluralists" are those who saw factions but not closed groups; and "populists" perceive a completely open party without factions or closed groups of decision-makers. Almost all of the ninety-three that could be typed fell into either the "pluralist" or "populist" property spaces.

TABLE 19

VIEW OF THE NATIONAL LIBERATION PARTY

Belief that Party has Internal Factions	Belief that Party is Run by Closed Group	
	Yes	No
Yes	Oligarchs (15)	Pluralists (41)
No	Establishmentarians (5)	Populists (32)

Although not statistically significant, the results of the cross-tabulation tended to point up that local leaders, not national leaders, view the PLN with greater "populism"; consequently, the opposite of the hypothesis *appears* to be true. However, this perception is undoubtedly due to the fact that local leaders, who are not intimately connected with the affairs of the national party, are not as aware that factions exist. On the other hand, national leaders witness day-to-day activities and take greater notice of cleavages.

In conclusion, it appears that local leaders do differ from national leaders both in background and outlook. Nationals are upper-middle-class, well-educated individuals with high-status occupations. They were more politicized at the time of joining the party, have remained ideologically oriented, and do not accept authoritarian notions. Locals, on the other hand, tend to come from lower-middle-class and working-class homes (although they are seldom of the working class themselves), are less educated, and hold lower status jobs. They are more interested in the "power" aspects of politics (winning elections, getting government jobs, gaining prestige); they are also noticeably more authoritarian and less ideological. In most respects the intermediate "liaison leaders" exhibit behavior patterns very similar to the national leaders. All and all, the claim of the PLN that it is the party of and for the common man, seeking to integrate him into the political life of the nation, has a certain authenticity, for national leaders do not appear to be recruiting persons exactly like themselves.

The Nature of Intrastructural Rivalry

This section deals with hypothetical structures and counter-structures and assumes that at every level of organization there exist both formal structures (i.e., the recognized "legal" party leaders) and opposite counterstructures of rival leaders. If this hypothesis proves true, an additional hypothesis will be presented: that each of the rival structures at the national level maintains loyal structures at the local levels which support it on questions of policy and in intraparty elections. It is assumed that some formal local structures are loyal to other-than-the-formal leadership structures at the national level and, vice versa, that the formal national structure is supported by counterstructures in some localities.

Most leaders recognized the existence of counterstructures at the national level. When presented with the item: "Almost all large political parties in the world today have divisions and internal groups that oppose each other at conventions, conferences, and so forth. Do you believe the National Liberation Party has these types of divisions?" 61 per cent of the 103 respondents replied in the affirmative. Also, those who recognized the existence of factions were agreed on the nature of the split; 84.6 per cent described a "leftist-conservative" dichotomy that divided certain national leaders against others. Most often mentioned as leader of the "progressive" or "leftist" wing was 1966 presidential candidate Daniel Oduber, supported by Luis Alberto Monge, Fernando Volio, José Luis Molina, and Alfonso Carro. The chief spokesman of the "conservative" wing appeared to be ex-President Francisco Orlich, aided by Jaime Solera, Gonzalo Facio, Francisco Garron, and the "business elements" within the PLN.[19] The most interesting fact is that few of the leaders perceiving divisions believed José Figueres was in any way involved; 90.9 per cent either stated that don Pepe was some kind of "balance" between the two intraparty forces or was not involved at all. Only four leaders believed him affiliated with either faction. Figueres' image as the great caudillo of the *entire* party was still untarnished in late 1965 and early 1966 when the poll was taken. It has been noted that he lost that image by alienating many leftists during the 1967–70 period.

A follow-up question sought to establish whether such divisions were basically ideological in nature or simply cases of ins versus outs. When asked "Would you say that the primary

TABLE 20

"OVER WHAT TYPE OF ISSUES DO PARTY DIVISIONS
BECOME MOST HEATED?"

	Per Cent	(n)
Questions of social welfare and social justice	26.2	16
Control of party machinery	24.6	15
Questions of state regulation of private business	21.3	13
Elections of party officers	13.1	8
Questions of economic development	8.2	5
Attitudes toward communism	3.3	2
Other ideology-oriented responses	6.5	4
Other power-oriented responses	0.0	0

controversies between the factions are purely ideological or based on the personal merits of certain leaders against others?" 44.4 per cent of those answering said the divisions were purely ideological, 28.9 per cent stated they were based mostly on personal differences, and 26.7 per cent believed they were based on a combination of both. Most interviewees were quite positive about the issues which cause the greatest amount of internal division. Table 20 lists the general types of issues most frequently offered by those who admitted the existence of such divisions. Again, multiple responses were given in several instances, so the total cannot equal 100.0 per cent.

After establishing the probable existence of regular factions at the national level, some information was obtained concerning

19. In addition to those describing the Oduber-Orlich split, 7.7 per cent mentioned the 1958 Rossi division and 7.7 per cent considered yet other types.

their existence at the local levels. The sample was drawn in such a manner that if factions did exist at the lower levels, rival leaders would also be included. A method was employed whereby lists of current officers were matched against the evaluation of local persons. Upon entering the localities, the author asked a number of persons (usually seven or eight) who they considered to be the most important PLN leaders in the community. Surprising agreement was found, both between the responses of different persons and between those responses and the formal lists. In other words, local persons not only knew who the formal party leaders were, but recognized them as the "real" leaders within their communities. Even when names were mentioned that were not on the lists, it usually turned out that the persons had recently been party officers but had voluntarily retired for various reasons. No evidence was uncovered by this method to support the hypothesis that networks of countergroups exist at local levels. Likewise, when questioned directly about the existence of small groups of party leaders "that make the majority of decisions of the party" at the local level, only 27.3 per cent of the fifty-five local leaders felt such groups existed. Most were not referring to their own localities, however, but to very rural places where caciques still run the party. Factionalizing does not seem to be a phenomenon at the local level. This is probably due to the fact that local units are dormant three years out of four and local leaders do not work together with enough regularity to form cliques.

Although factions do not seem to appear at the local level, several questions were included to ascertain whether or not national factions communicate with local leaders in any regular fashion. An attempt was made to discern which of the two large national factions appealed most to local respondents and by this method obtain some insights into patterns of national-local structural alliances. Only twenty-three of the fifty-five local leaders acknowledged the existence of factions at any level, but of those twenty-three the vast majority believed the Oduber wing was more popular in the locality (see Table 21). The strong preference for the Oduber wing was undoubtedly misleading, however, for the respondents were asked to choose between two wings at the precise time that the leader of one was the party's presidential candidate, and partisan propaganda bearing his likeness was in abundance across the nation. With enthusiasm at such a fever pitch, it is quite possible (and altogether too probable) that many respondents offered Oduber's name out of party loyalty. After all, how many United States Democratic county committeemen would have stated that Eugene McCarthy was more popular than Hubert Humphrey in the fall of 1968?

Also, local leaders seem to hold their positions by a combination of seniority *and* approval from above. It has been noted that the local machinery becomes dormant after every election and has to be rebuilt in time for the next one four years later, utilizing, of course, the previous base as much as possible. Hence, the next presidential candidate (who is generally known at least a year prior to the election) can "rebuild" the party in such a fashion as to eliminate many of his local enemies, subject, of course, to Figueres' overall approval. In other words, the

TABLE 21

"WHICH OF THE VARIOUS PARTY WINGS YOU HAVE JUST
DESCRIBED IS MORE POPULAR AMONG YOUR FRIENDS
AND NEIGHBORS HERE IN_____?"

	Per Cent
Progressive wing led by Oduber and others	82.6
Conservative wing led by Orlich and others	13.0
Center wing led by Figueres	4.3
Total	99.9
(n)	(23)

sequence of events is something like this: The new presidential candidate (who may not yet have been formally "elected" by the PLN National Congress) looks around and finds a sleeping party at the local levels. The majority of local leaders from the last election will not normally be identified with either of the two national ideological factions and can easily be asked to assume their old (or comparable) positions, providing they had done a respectable job in the past. Others will have moved away or become disinterested, so the presidential candidate can replace them with allies or neutrals. Consequently, only a relative few will normally be considered foes, and some of them can be won over by flattery, threats, or promises of patronage. Some of the more intransigent types can be shunted aside and replaced by more cooperative persons. Consequently, a small minority will ultimately prove too entrenched to be ousted or bought off. Of course, all leaders have to be elected by local party assemblies at the appropriate level, but this seldom poses a problem since the assemblies do not function effectively in most areas. The presidential candidate, then, is virtually guaranteed the friendship of the local machinery. This factor also accounts for the low number of Oduber-dislikers found in the sample.

On the basis of these data the hypothesis has to be rejected. Although factions do appear at the national level, no evidence of their regular existence was discovered at the local levels. Furthermore, there was no evidence that national factions appeal to local leaders in any systematic way or that national leadership structures maintain local structures which regularly give support and backing. One may believe that a number of alternative local leaders exist who may retain greater preferences for other candidates, but their existence does not necessarily suggest regular and permanent dichotomies at the local levels.

LaPalombara and Weiner's second criterion is unquestionably met. Since 1951 the PLN has maintained an increasingly complex network of neighborhood, district, and cantonal committees and assemblies, plus several auxiliary organizations, including the Juventud Liberacionista youth movement, which itself maintains a modest set of local units. Local leaders, especially those at the cantonal level, actively promote the party's candidates, communicate more or less regularly with immediate superiors in the party, and tend to hold their positions over several campaign periods. They do not, however, function as members of a team between elections. In terms of social and attitudinal differences, national leaders tend to be more cosmopolitan, politicized, better educated, upper-middle-class individuals with notably less "power" orientation and authoritarianism. Locals are more lower-middle-class (but seldom working-class), more authoritarian, less ideological, and less politicized. They tend to be in politics for its rewards or for the "fun" of it and show less tendency to want to change things.

6. National Liberation Support in Four Elections

I N THIS CHAPTER we consider the third and fourth of La-
Palombara and Weiner's criteria together. Partisan efforts
to control decision-making apparatuses *and* the acquisition
of popular support are both intimately interconnected with
elections in democratic politics; Costa Rica, since the early
1950's, has experienced a series of meaningful elections.
Voting turnout in 1953, 1958, 1962, and 1966 is examined and a
number of hypotheses relating to the nature of PLN support are
presented. A brief overview will first be necessary to acquaint
the reader with the National Liberation electoral position
relative to other political groups in the nation.[1]

1. Unfortunately, very little academically sound material has been published
concerning recent elections; Costa Rican literature on the subject is, for the most
part, extremely partisan in nature with little attempted analysis. Only a few
noteworthy studies dealing specifically with elections have been published to
date. See Harry Kantor, *The Costa Rican Election of 1953: A Case Study*; and
two works by Paul G. Stephenson, *Costa Rican Election Factbook, February 6,
1966* and "Costa Rican Government and Politics." Also see, John Yochelson,
"What Price Political Stability? The 1966 Presidential Campaign in Costa Rica,"
Public and International Affairs, pp. 279–307; and John D. Martz, "Costa Rican
Electoral Trends, 1953–1966," *The Western Political Quarterly*, pp. 888–909.

An Overview of the Four Elections[2]

The campaign of 1953 was the first instance in which the major contemporary parties, greatly realigned as a result of the 1948 war, opposed each other in electoral competition at the presidential level. The PLN National Congress of 1952 unanimously nominated José Figueres, and he led the new party to the polls. The opposition included different political groupings of varying beliefs and persuasions, united in one goal only—to stop Figueres. The Democratic Party (PD),[3] temporarily created in order to present a presidential candidate acceptable to all divergent factions, provided the only competition. The PD was in Professor Kantor's words:"... an *ad hoc* organization created especially for the 1953 campaign. It confined within its ranks most of the large landowners, the majority of the businessmen, and most of those who for various reasons disliked the National Liberation Party and its leader José Figueres."[4] An uncontroversial businessman, Fernando Castro Cervantes, was chosen to represent the coalition at the polls.[5]

The National Union Party (PUN), unable to renominate its constitutionally ineligible leader and founder, President Otilio Ulate, chose Mario Echandi, who ultimately withdrew in favor of Castro. Although supposedly one of the strongest parties in national politics at the time, old rivalries dating from the early forties made it virtually impossible for the PUN to coalesce the outside support it would have needed to attain another presidential victory. Likewise, Rafael Calderón's Republican Party (PRN) was unable to offer a presidential nominee due to the fact that many of its leaders, including Calderón himself, were still in exile. A group of former Calderón supporters campaigning

2. The reader is referred to Figure 1 for a visual overview of the coalition patterns during this period.

3. Although the name was the same as the Democratic, or Cortesista, Party of the 1942–48 period, it was in almost no way the same group. The old PD had virtually ceased to function after its leader, ex-President Leon Cortes (1936–40), died in 1947. During the realignment period of 1948–53, many, probably a majority, of its former leaders joined Figueres in founding the new PLN; others gravitated toward Ulatismo. In 1953 only a few of the former PD leaders participated in the newly created Democratic Party.

4. Kantor, *Costa Rican Election*, p. 35.

5. It will be remembered that Castro had earlier been the leader of the school of thought within the anti-Calderón opposition during the 1946–48 period which favored cooperation with the Calderón government. As such, he had relatively few political enemies and could be supported by Calderonista and anti-Calderonista alike.

under the name Independent National Republican Party (PRNI) nominated candidates for the legislature and local municipal councils in the province of San José; in other areas, Calderonistas were urged to support the PD.

The Communist Popular Vanguard Party (PVP) had been outlawed as an agent of a foreign government by Figueres' revolutionary junta in 1949, but a hastily organized front organization, the Independent Progressive Party (PPI), attained official recognition in 1952. Although it supported the opposition's presidential candidate and actively campaigned for its own legislative and municipal candidates, the Legislative Assembly revoked recognition just two days before the election.

The electoral results surprised almost no one. Figueres won a nearly two-to-one victory, beating his opponent 123,444 to 67,324. The PLN also received 114,043 out of a total 176,130 legislative votes, with the PD, PRNI, and PUN dividing the remainder: 37,322, 12,696, and 12,069, respectively.[6]

However, the mandate of 1953 did not last. All opposition parties united behind the PUN's Echandi in time for the 1958 election; simultaneously, a number of PLN leaders led by Jorge Rossi temporarily left the party to form the Independent Party (PI). As a result, Francisco Orlich, the Liberation candidate, received only 43 per cent of the total valid vote. Even if the totals of the PI are added to the PLN's vote on the assumption that an absence of internal strife would have put the PI's vote in the PLN column, the result is slightly less than 54 per cent—still a far cry from Figueres' 63 per cent just four years earlier. National Liberation proved itself the strongest *single* party in the nation, however, by obtaining 86,081 legislative votes to the PR's 46,171 and the PUN's 44,125. Municipal council seats were divided almost evenly between the PLN and all other contesting parties.

In addition to the PI, five small personalist groups entered candidates for the legislative race. Only the Civic Revolutionary Union Party (PUCR) deserves mention, because it has maintained itself as a coherent force, dedicated since 1957 to the ambitions of its hero and founder, Frank Marshall, a former PLN military commander.

6. All electoral statistics used in this chapter were obtained directly from the official records of the Supreme Tribunal of Elections, San José. It will be noted that the Calderón-oriented PRNI with a makeshift organizational structure received more votes in the province of San José alone than the PUN did in the entire nation.

By 1962 the division in the PLN had been resolved, and all internal factions supported Orlich's second candidacy. Moreover, the major opposition parties each nominated separate presidential candidates; the PRN ran Calderón while the PUN nominated Ulate. The Communists, meanwhile, supported a fourth hopeful, ex-liberacionista Enrique Obregón Valverde, whose pro-Fidel-Castro Popular Democratic Action Party (PADP) was widely considered another front for Manuel Mora's illegal PVP. The campaign quickly developed into a two-way contest between Orlich and Calderón because Ulate had apparently lost much of his former appeal, and extreme leftist Obregón never had a chance.

In the first Costa Rican election demanding universal obligatory voting[7] the PLN won, receiving 50.3 per cent of the total valid vote. Calderón proved his popularity by obtaining slightly over 35 per cent. Ulate and the PUN received an embarrassing 13.5 per cent, while the PADP obtained an insignificant nine-tenths of 1 per cent. Out of a total of nine parties contesting the legislative race, the PLN received 184,135 out of 376,937 votes, or 49 per cent. Due to Costa Rica's system of proportional representation, however, that figure was sufficient to give it a one-seat absolute majority in the Legislative Assembly, 29–28. Again, seats on local municipal councils were divided nearly evenly between the PLN and all other parties.

The 1962 election tended to point up several factors. First, the PLN, whose leaders had originally taken control in 1948 with overwhelming and genuine popular enthusiasm and whose presidential candidate had received almost two-thirds of the national presidential vote in 1953, could only count on the regular support of about half of Costa Rica's voters in any given election a decade later. Second, Ulate, and probably the PUN as a whole, could never again hope to see victory apart from a coalition with other major opposition parties (i.e., the PRN). Third, the Republicans and their *jefe*, Rafael Calderón Guardia, had displayed amazing strength after fourteen years in the political shadows and could be counted upon to provide effective competition in future elections.

The National Liberation Party maintained outward unity from 1962 to 1966. Although no separate splinter groups of counter-

7. A constitutional provision of 1959 authorized the Supreme Tribunal of Elections to impose fines on persons refusing to vote.

elites formed a separate party as in 1958, dissension grew between the "leftist" and "conservative" wings of the party. Daniel Oduber, generally considered a leader of the left, was nominated presidential candidate by the 1965 Party Congress, and there appeared to be some evidence that many conservatives failed to actively support his campaign. The PRN and PUN not only supported a single presidential candidate, Professor José Joaquin Trejos, under the banner of the newly created (1965) National Unification Party (PUN₁),[8] but for the first time merged their individual campaign machinery and nominated a single merged list of candidates for municipal council seats. Frank Marshall's PUCR tacitly supported the PUN₁.

A central issue of the campaign involved Oduber's alleged Communist inclinations. Opposition propaganda charged that the PLN under Oduber had become dangerously pro-Communist, and a letter to Mora, bearing Oduber's signature and requesting support in return for certain favors, was printed in major newspapers. Although Oduber and other PLN leaders strongly denied the letter and labeled it a forgery, a significant number of party leaders interviewed indicated that the charge was partly responsible for the party's defeat.

When the votes were counted, the opposition had won by only 4,220, less than 1 per cent of the total 451,490. Although the PLN received 49.3 per cent of the total valid votes cast in the legislative race to the PUN₁'s 46.3 per cent, adding to the latter the 3.3 per cent received by the PUCR brought the two forces into equal balance.[9] Again, municipal council seats were divided evenly. On the eve of the 1970 election the PUN-PRN merger is still intact although extremely tenuous;[10] nevertheless, the two

8. The subscript is appended to the National Unification Party's initials only to distinguish it from the National Union Party. Another small group, the Authentic Republican Union Party, also joined the coalition but was too small to merit further comment.

9. The remaining few tenths of 1 per cent were obtained by three small provincial parties.

10. Soon after the 1966 election the PUN and the PRN established separate floor organizations in the Legislative Assembly, and the cabinet of President Trejos was rife with political rifts. Although some of the cleavage was personal in nature, overtones of old Ulatista-Calderonista rivalries were omnipresent. In addition, controversy over the choice of the 1970 presidential candidate further jeopardized the future of the National Unification Party. No political neutral acceptable to both factions emerged as in 1966; consequently, each supported a favorite. Ulatistas coalesced behind former President Mario Echandi (1958–62) while a number of Calderonistas supported Virgilio Calvo. Calderón

major political forces seem to command nearly identical "permanent" strength at the polls. Consequently, future victories shall hinge on two factors: the ability of either party to avoid splinter factions running as separate parties (e.g., Jorge Rossi's Independent Party in 1958 or Virgilio Calvo's Third Front in 1970) *or* the behavior of small third parties such as Frank Marshall's PUCR in 1966. The growth of PLN strength has been largely responsible for the creation of a countersystem with roughly equivalent structure and differentiation.

In conclusion to this overview, there is no question that the third of LaPalombara and Weiner's criteria is met. The PLN has entered all electoral campaigns since 1953 and its leaders have tried very hard to win. The reasons it has been successful at some times and not at others will now be considered.

Explanations of National Liberation Party Successes and Failures

The 103 party leaders were asked to explain why their party lost certain elections and won others. The interview items were straightforward: "Why do you believe the National Liberation Party won the elections of 1953 and 1962?" and "Why do you believe the party lost the election of 1958?"[11] Since the questions were open-ended a considerable number of different responses were expressed, but they tended to fall into several categories and could be coded into six to nine types per election.

Sixty-two per cent of those who ventured opinions about their party's victory in 1953 agreed that the popularity of candidate José Figueres was an important factor. A similar 58 per cent believed the party's program and ideology were also important. It must be noted, however, that since the image of Figueres was so charismatically interwoven with the aims of the 1948 revolution and overall liberacionista ideology in the minds of many

---

subsequently angered many of his admirers by publicly endorsing Echandi, thereby securing the PUN₁ nomination for the former chief executive. Calvo later formed a Third Front to promote his candidacy on a separate ticket, splitting the electoral support of PLN's opposition.

11. After the February 6, 1966, election the second question was changed to: "Why do you believe the party lost the elections of 1958 and 1966?" Since 81 of the total 103 party leaders were interviewed after that date, most responses include opinions for all four elections. Ninety-four responses were tallied for the 1953 and 1962 elections; ninety-two for the 1958 election; and seventy-two for the 1966 election. Many times interviewees gave multiple responses to the question, so percentages cannot total 100 per cent.

party regulars, it was often difficult to determine whether respondents were referring to the former or the latter. One local leader from the province of Alajuela stated in typical fashion: "Don Pepe gave the nation a new start in 1948 when he abolished the army and took control of the banks away from the rich people." Another from a rural canton in San José province pinpointed the tendency to associate the image of Figueres with the party's program and ideology even more clearly: "Figuerismo did more for Costa Rica in a year and a half than all the politicians had done in a century and a half." These are only two of several dozens of responses which revealed that to many of his supporters don Pepe was the physical embodiment of PLN ideology.

Few leaders felt that additional factors contributed greatly to the 1953 victory. Although the PLN was unquestionably the most highly organized of the electoral contestants, only 7 per cent gave this as a prime factor. Three per cent stated the PLN had won because the 1949–53 administration of President Otilio Ulate had been "weak" or "bad," and 2 per cent believed hatred of former President Calderón was so intense that Figueres was elected because he had been the chief instrument of Calderón's downfall.

Responses concerning the victory of 1962 are notably different, for no one confused the candidate with party program. Only 19 per cent believed Francisco Orlich's popularity was a factor, while 53 per cent agreed ideology was important. In fact, 16 per cent of those who rendered ideology as a factor felt that Orlich somehow detracted from overall party strength. "Orlich was only able to win," grumbled one national leader residing in the capital, "because Figueres had done so much before him."[12] "Don Chico [Orlich] could not have won by himself; the party won it for him," declared a district committeeman in Heredia. In a similar vein, 20 per cent stated victory had been due to superior organization and 23 per cent confided that victory came only because opposition parties could not form a coalition as they had in 1953 and 1958. Thirty-one per cent felt that the 1958–62 Echandi administration was so bad that PLN victory was virtually guaranteed.

Almost everyone (89 per cent) believed organizational factors

12. The respondent then went on to explain how he believed Orlich had "stabbed the party in the back" after he became president.

were responsible for defeat in 1958. Of that number, most (85 per cent) felt defeat was primarily due to Jorge Rossi's defection and subsequent candidacy on the Independent Party ticket; only 4 per cent ventured the opinion that the "other" party was more highly organized. An additional 4 per cent implied that Orlich's candidacy was responsible and 3 per cent believed PLN program and ideology were at fault. A significant 10 per cent agreed that the record of Figueres' 1953–58 term contributed to the defeat; 6 per cent blamed "unfortunate and uncontrollable setbacks" (the drop in coffee prices after the Korean War, et cetera); and 4 per cent blamed Figueres personally. Again, the vast majority maintained or implied that had Rossi's faction not bolted, victory would have been attained. Many cited the fact that combined votes for Orlich and Rossi surpassed the opposition total.

Those questioned about the 1966 election explained the party's defeat in terms similar to 1958. More than two-thirds (69 per cent) gave some form of organizational response: the opposition was more highly organized, 7 per cent; too much apathy and disunity within PLN ranks, 39 per cent;[13] the party was too overconfident, 18 per cent. Only 8 per cent felt candidate Daniel Oduber was unpopular, and only 1 per cent blamed the party's platform. Ten per cent were of the opinion that the preceding Orlich administration had been a failure and had hurt the party at the polls, while an additional 10 per cent credited the opposition charge of Communist infiltration with the defeat. It is interesting to note the apparent lack of credence granted the national leadership's charge of fraud. Although candidate Oduber had televised a nationwide speech several days after the election, insisting his defeat was due to electoral malpractices, and the PLN National Directory had issued a public statement to the same effect, only 9 per cent of those interviewed listed the charge as a prime factor. Many openly stated that the charge of fraud was a cover-up and excuse.

In conclusion, the above opinions testify that the PLN leaders interviewed upheld, for the most part, the vote-getting qualities of their party's ideology, programs, platforms, and candidates. They tended to blame weakness in organization or morale for the two defeats. A follow-up question, "What do you suggest in

13. Of the 39 per cent, 25 per cent specifically mentioned that members of the party's conservative wing had not vigorously supported the candidate.

order to insure the party future victories?" tended to support general response patterns. Table 22 illustrates that a majority felt the organizational machinery of the party needed attention.

TABLE 22

SUGGESTIONS FOR FUTURE VICTORIES

	Per Cent
Ideological	17
Provide better government	18
Strengthen party machinery	61
Other	4
Total	100

The Stability of the Support Base

Although the PLN has won two of the four Costa Rican elections, its percentages of the total valid vote in those elections has been progressively lower as Table 23 demonstrates. These data seem to suggest that the great coalition created by Figueres and the Generation of '48 in the early 1950's has been undergoing some sort of steady change. If such change has been taking place, it has affected both presidential and legislative support, not only because the legislative percentage has decreased in the same ratio as the presidential percentage, but because there is an extremely strong relationship between presidential and legislative support in any given single year (see Table 24), indicating that "ticket-splitting" is virtually nonexistent. By correlating the cantonal percentages of the total valid vote received by the PLN in the four presidential elections to its percentages in the legislative election of the same years,[14] it was discovered that the cantons that support the party's presidential candidate support

14. Pearson's Product-Moment Correlation was employed to measure the relationship between any two variables in this chapter. A correlation coefficient (r) is a mathematical statement about the vertical distance of the individuals (in this case cantons) from a "line of best fit." An r of 0.0 signifies the individuals are widely scattered and no relation exists, but as it increases toward either 1.0 or −1.0, the relationship becomes progressively stronger, either positively or negatively. An analysis of variance test was used to test for significance; since the number of cantons is the same for all correlations in the chapter, the r needed for significance (±0.244) at the 0.05 level is also the same. Where space permits, the notation sig. is placed beside significant r's for the convenience of the reader. As in chapters 4 and 5, all relationships described as significant had less than five chances in a hundred to come about randomly.

its legislative list as well (although this seems to have been somewhat less true in 1966).

TABLE 23

NATIONAL LIBERATION PARTY
PERCENTAGE OF TOTAL
VALID VOTE, 1953–66

Year	President (per cent)	Legislative (per cent)
1953	64.7	64.8
1958	53.6*	51.5*
1962	50.3	48.9
1966	49.5	49.3

*This percentage includes the votes of the dissident PLN leadership faction that campaigned as the Independent Party.

TABLE 24

RELATIONSHIP BETWEEN
NATIONAL LIBERATION
PARTY PRESIDENTIAL
AND LEGISLATIVE
SUPPORT, 1953–66

Year	r
1953	0.968 (sig.)
1958	0.958 (sig.)
1962	0.992 (sig.)
1966	0.868 (sig.)

The question at this point is whether the PLN is losing relative support randomly or whether the base itself is undergoing change in a systematic fashion. By correlating the PLN percentages of the 1966 election with the percentages of each of the three other elections, it can be seen that the coefficients become progressively smaller, thus lending some support to the hypothesis that the party's base of popular support is shifting through time. However, since the decrease in the coefficients (Table 25) is not great, the data are not conclusive.

One hypothetical explanation for the decreases in the r's in Table 25 involves opposition activity following its devastating defeat in 1953. If the "other" party[15] saw the handwriting on the wall and realized that to compete in the future it would have to mobilize the masses, it is possible that the apparent shift in PLN support could simply be a reflection of that mobilization, and the progressive decrease in the PLN's national percentage would be

15. The reader is left to decide how to define the second party in Costa Rican politics. Since the PRN and the PUN were in coalition in three of the last four elections, it is difficult to ascertain which of the two might be responsible for activity resulting in the change of voting patterns. One could conceptualize the "other" party in 1958 and 1966 as: (1) the PRN by itself, (2) the PUN by itself, (3) the PRN with PUN assistance, (4) the PUN with PRN assistance, or (5) the two working together on a basis of equality. The author prefers the third concept because the popular appeal of PRN is much greater than that of the PUN as demonstrated in the 1962 election.

partially explained as well. If the other party did make a determined effort to gain support across the nation, a substantial negative correlation should exist between the cantons whose percentage of the total valid vote increased greatly between 1953 and 1958 and the PLN percentage in 1958 (which in a two party election would mean that the other party would correlate positively to the same degree). Although the correlation (-0.239)

TABLE 25

1966 NATIONAL LIBERATION PARTY
VOTE AND PRECEDING ELECTIONS

Year	Presidential r	Legislative r
1966	1.000	1.000
1962	0.833	0.874
1958	0.801	0.797
1953	0.726	0.612

TABLE 26

VOTING TURNOUT, 1953–66

Year	Estimated Eligible Voters	Percentage of Eligible Voters that Voted
1953	398,372	47.9
1958	439,032	50.5
1962	471,560	81.3
1966	504,088	89.6

was not statistically significant, it came very close; under the circumstances the hypothesis could not be totally rejected.

The second possible explanation for the apparent change in electoral support is that the compulsory voting act of 1959 forced new types of voters to the polls in 1962. If those types tended to support the opposition more than the PLN, the downward trend of the PLN's coefficients as well as the percentages would also be better explained. Unquestionably, compulsory voting has drastically increased electoral turnout. Table 26 demonstrates that the percentage of eligible voters (all persons over the age of twenty) that voted stayed about the same between 1953 and 1958, but jumped in 1962, the election following the 1959 law, and remained at the higher level in 1966. The electoral percentages of all three major parties in 1962 were correlated to the cantonal percentages of increase between 1958 and 1962, but the results were not significant as Table 27 demonstrates.

Therefore, the "reluctant voters" that had to be forced to the polls seem to have exhibited greater preference for the PRN, but the hypothesis had to be rejected for lack of significance.

As a final check, 1962–66 cantonal percentages of increase were correlated with the PLN's cantonal percentages in 1966. If a significant negative r existed, it could be argued that opposition mobilization affected the last of the four elections. Although

TABLE 27

EFFECTS OF THE COMPULSORY VOTING LAW ON THE
SUPPORT BASES OF THE THREE MAJOR PARTIES IN
1962: PERCENTAGES OF PARTY VOTES IN 1962
RELATING TO THE INCREASE IN ELECTORAL
TURNOUT, 1958–62

Party	r
National Liberation Party	−0.101
National Republican Party	0.198
National Union Party	−0.210

it would not explain the downward shift of the r's between 1953 and 1962, it could have some bearing on the overall trend. On the other hand if the r were positive, it could be argued that the PLN made an even more determined effort to bring in new types of voters between 1962 and 1966, thus shifting the base.[16] In any event, the relation was not significant (−0.068) and the hypothesis was rejected.

To conclude this section, the central hypothesis, *that the base of National Liberation Party popular support is undergoing slow but gradual change*, still cannot be rejected although it appears the opposition did make an attempt to mobilize the masses in 1958. The next section will analyze the effects of eleven hypothetically relevant variables on that base of support and on the nature of the change, if any.

The Effects of Major Socioeconomic Variables

Eleven demographic and economic variables were correlated to the PLN's percentage of the total valid vote, by canton, in each of the eight elections described above (four presidential and

16. The continued downward trend of its total national percentage would still not be explained under the second alternative, but it might then be argued that elements of the original supporting types resented the PLN's catering to others and voted for the opposition.

four legislative). If the PLN's base of support has been undergoing a steady shift, and if the eleven variables are relevant, those variables that correlated relatively high at the beginning should correlate low or not at all (or perhaps even in an opposite manner in extreme cases) several elections later, while variables that correlated low at the beginning should correlate higher toward the end. It must be kept in mind that Costa Rican cantons, like United States counties, are relatively large geographical areas containing many types of individuals. Although some are more agricultural, commercial, industrial, and so on than others, most have their own landowners, taxi drivers, shopkeepers, peasants, salaried employees, businessmen, and others who presumably vote their individual interests. Therefore, very high correlation coefficients cannot be expected, and relatively low degrees (such as .3 or .4) are considered meaningful *if clear and consistent patterns emerge* election after election. At the same time, it is admitted that mass aggregate data describing units so complex and heterogeneous can be misleading.[17] Unfortunately, neither Costa Rican voting procedures nor present methods of census reporting make analysis of smaller and more homogeneous units possible.

Land Ownership.[18]—The PLN has always portrayed itself as the protector of the small farmer. It has aimed its campaigns toward him and has sponsored certain economic programs designed to benefit him. Presumably, then, cantons with widespread ownership would tend to support the PLN because of the high percentage of small farmers. No pattern emerged, however,

17. See W. S. Robinson's controversial "Ecological Correlations and the Behavior of Individuals," *American Sociological Review*, pp. 351–57.

18. The concept of landownership was operationalized by dividing the number of farms per canton into the number of agricultural workers. The implication is that, as the dividend increases, the percentage of those owning their own farms decreases. Ideally, one worker per farm would show perfect distribution (minifundia), and many workers per farm would show a condition of manor or plantation farming (latifundia). The operation does not take into account two obvious possibilities: (1) a few wealthy landowners might own many separate farms which although run as one large unit would show up in census reports as separate units, or (2) many agricultural workers might not actually *own* their land but simply rent from wealthier neighbors. Unfortunately, available data did not permit these possibilities to be controlled. The cantons ranged from 1.9 workers per farm (Buenos Aires of Puntarenas) to 8.2 (Jimenez of Cartago). Although San José Central had a ratio of 12.9, the high degree of urbanity of the canton (99 per cent of the population is considered urban) properly disqualifies it from consideration.

and the hypothesis was rejected. Table 28 illustrates that under the definition, no significant relation existed.

Upper-White-Collar Workers.[19] — Since the PLN describes itself as a "popular party" with a wide base of support, it might be assumed that no or little correlation exists between electoral strength and class-oriented variables. This, however, does not seem to be the case; a moderate but consistent negative

TABLE 28

LAND OWNERSHIP

Election		r
Presidential	1953	0.129
Congressional	1953	0.163
Presidential	1958	−0.093
Congressional	1958	−0.174
Presidential	1962	−0.177
Congressional	1962	−0.197
Presidential	1966	−0.020
Congressional	1966	−0.113

TABLE 29

UPPER-WHITE-COLLAR WORKERS

Election		r
Presidential	1953	−0.191
Congressional	1953	−0.149
Presidential	1958	−0.391 (sig.)
Congressional	1958	−0.424 (sig.)
Presidential	1962	−0.398 (sig.)
Congressional	1962	−0.425 (sig.)
Presidential	1966	−0.362 (sig.)
Congressional	1966	−0.342 (sig.)

connection has existed between the two since 1958. Since no correlation existed in 1953, this variable could partially explain the apparent shift in the PLN support base, but the increase is not gradual and continuous as the shift. Therefore, the data are inconclusive and judgment cannot be made at this time. Nevertheless, since 1958, cantons with high percentages of upper-white-collar workers do not support the PLN as Table 29 demonstrates.

19. Professionals, technicians, and administrative managers. The percentage of these occupation types in the total work force was correlated to the dependent variables by canton. The same technique was employed for the other occupational groups in this chapter as well.

Lower-White-Collar Workers.[20] — National Liberation Party strategists have tried hardest to capture the support of this occupational group, and it might be expected that cantons with high percentages of lower-white-collar workers might ameliorate the effects of upper-white-collar cantons. However, Table 30 indicates that lower-white-collar cantons do not support the party any more than upper-white-collar cantons do. Again, the PLN gained these cantons randomly in 1953; thus this variable also tends to support the contention concerning support shift. However, like the previous variable the increase in *r* was not gradual as expected but abrupt, beginning in 1958. Judgment must also be held temporarily.

TABLE 30

LOWER-WHITE-COLLAR WORKERS

Election		*r*
Presidential	1953	-0.095
Congressional	1953	-0.020
Presidential	1958	-0.360 (sig.)
Congressional	1958	-0.452 (sig.)
Presidential	1962	-0.391 (sig.)
Congressional	1962	-0.434 (sig.)
Presidential	1966	-0.272 (sig.)
Congressional	1966	-0.343 (sig.)

Agricultural Workers. — The National Liberation Party has incorporated representatives of this group into its lower leadership cadres in an attempt to gain support among those traditionally most deprived of political participation. Therefore, it might be hypothesized that cantons containing great percentages of rural workers would tend to vote heavily in the party's favor. Table 31 indicates that such cantons do indeed correlate with PLN turnout in a positive manner almost exactly as white-collar cantons do negatively. Again the change was abrupt not gradual.

This variable should have been controlled by distinguishing between two distinct types of agricultural workers in Costa Rica. The larger category contains those who work in the traditional coffee and vegetable farms of the Meseta Central or in the cattle

20. The percentages of office employees and sales persons in the total work force were correlated to the dependent variables.

TABLE 31

AGRICULTURAL WORKERS

Election		r
Presidential	1953	0.012
Congressional	1953	0.095
Presidential	1958	0.447 (sig.)
Congressional	1958	0.352 (sig.)
Presidential	1962	0.409 (sig.)
Congressional	1962	0.446 (sig.)
Presidential	1966	0.317 (sig.)
Congressional	1966	0.388 (sig.)

ranches and cotton fields of Guanacaste. As a group, these workers have benefited greatly from PLN administrations. Members of the second group, centered entirely in the provinces of Limón and Puntarenas, work in the large foreign-owned banana plantations and are much more politically organized through their trade unions. As a group they made certain gains during the 1943–48 period of Calderón-Communist collaboration, and most labor organizations in those provinces have been affiliated with the Communist PVP.[21] Consequently, it might be expected that holding this factor constant might yield somewhat different results. Table 32 illustrates the high degree of support for the PLN in the presidential elections from 1958 to 1966 in non-Puntarenas–Limón cantons with the highest concentrations on agricultural workers, and Table 33 shows an opposite voting pattern in similar cantons within those two provinces. Only the canton of Buenos Aires in Puntarenas exhibits a voting pattern

TABLE 32

NON-PUNTARENAS–LIMÓN CANTONS

Canton	Percentage of Work Force in Agriculture	Percentage of Vote for PLN		
		1958	1962	1966
Acosta	85.2	65.6	60.2	56.1
Turribares	83.7	51.5	63.9	51.7
Puriscal	82.7	66.4	67.9	62.5
Bagaces	81.9	62.5	62.1	54.3
Alvarado	81.2	73.8	65.4	61.5

21. Manuel Mora originally founded his party in 1929 as a movement to organize such workers against the United Fruit Company. See Robert J. Alexander, *Communism in Latin America*, pp. 383–91.

similar to cantons of the same type in other parts of the nation. This exception can be readily explained on the basis of geography and climate. This sparsely populated, upland region produces coffee and rice rather than bananas, and maintains an agricultural system *almost identical to the cantons in Table 32.* In conclusion, the data tend to prove that cantons with high concentrations of agricultural workers—except those with an agricultural system based on large foreign-owned plantations with unionized laborers—heavily support the National Liberation Party.

TABLE 33

PUNTARENAS-LIMÓN CANTONS

Canton	Percentage of Work Force in Agriculture	Percentage of Vote for PLN		
		1958	1962	1966
Buenos Aires	88.0	72.7	62.7	59.2
Poccoci	80.0	34.8	39.4	41.2
Montes de Oro	71.1	61.6	50.3	46.4
Siquirres	69.4	44.5	39.3	39.7
Golfito	60.6	35.6	34.2	40.4

TABLE 34

BLUE-COLLAR WORKERS

Election		r
Presidential	1953	− 0.097
Congressional	1953	− 0.014
Presidential	1958	− 0.286 (sig.)
Congressional	1958	− 0.385 (sig.)
Presidential	1962	− 0.356 (sig.)
Congressional	1962	− 0.386 (sig.)
Presidential	1966	− 0.274 (sig.)
Congressional	1966	− 0.348 (sig.)

Blue-Collar Workers.—Cantons with proportionally higher concentrations of miners, artisans, and industrial workers are undoubtedly more commercial and industrial in nature, and consequently less rural and traditional. Since PLN support seems to be centered in the less modern areas, it might be expected that such cantons would not normally support the party. By the same token, one could assume that areas of this type might normally support the Calderonista candidates since blue-collar workers as a group benefited economically from the Labor Code, minimum wage law, and other reforms of the Calderón government. As it turns out, there is indeed a consistent negative relationship as Table 34 demonstrates. Again, the change is not gradual as hypothesized; a weak correlation begins in 1958 and remains static thereafter.

Service Workers. — Persons employed as transport drivers, household workers, and others are found in the more urban centers, where relative affluence guarantees them greater job

TABLE 35

SERVICE WORKERS

Election		r
Presidential	1953	− 0.140
Congressional	1953	− 0.070
Presidential	1958	− 0.349 (sig.)
Congressional	1958	− 0.401 (sig.)
Presidential	1962	− 0.384 (sig.)
Congressional	1962	− 0.422 (sig.)
Presidential	1966	− 0.306 (sig.)
Congressional	1966	− 0.371 (sig.)

opportunities. The evidence thus far tends to support the thesis that urban centers do not support the National Liberation Party, and this indicator is no exception. Table 35 shows that since 1958, cantons with high percentages of service workers, like those with high percentages of white-collar and blue-collar workers, do not vote PLN as much as do rural, agricultural cantons. This variable behaved like the others regarding shifting popular support; the change was not gradual.

Education. — Developing nations generally maintain two educational standards: a relatively high one for the more affluent urban areas, and a much lower one for backward rural areas. While Costa Rica is somewhat of an exception to this general rule — widespread public school facilities were established far in advance of most Latin American nations — literacy is far greater in the cities than in the countryside. Consequently, the PLN should be particularly strong in cantons with low literacy. However, no pattern of significant coefficients was found between the two variables as Table 36 demonstrates.[22]

22. Illiteracy is defined as the percentage of persons over the age of twenty without more than three years of education.

Geographic Population Stability. — The number of persons that seek residence in a particular canton, either from elsewhere in the republic or from another nation, would presumably be a strong indicator of that canton's affluence, modernness, and relative opportunity. Highly rural, traditional, economically stagnant cantons would not attract new residents and would, in fact, lose proportional population as their more dynamic residents leave for urban centers. By calculating the percentage of persons born in their canton of residence and correlating that

TABLE 36

ILLITERACY

Election		r
Presidential	1953	− 0.040
Congressional	1953	− 0.073
Presidential	1958	0.148
Congressional	1958	0.243
Presidential	1962	0.242
Congressional	1962	0.262 (sig.)
Presidential	1966	0.102
Congressional	1966	0.191

TABLE 37

GEOGRAPHIC POPULATION STABILITY

Election		r
Presidential	1953	0.333 (sig.)
Congressional	1953	0.277 (sig.)
Presidential	1958	0.557 (sig.)
Congressional	1958	0.576 (sig.)
Presidential	1962	0.529 (sig.)
Congressional	1962	0.563 (sig.)
Presidential	1966	0.399 (sig.)
Congressional	1966	0.493 (sig.)

percentage to the PLN vote, a fairly clear picture of voting behavior is obtained. Table 37 illustrates a very significant positive relationship between the two variables. However, the gradual and continuous change predicted in the original hypothesis does not appear here either. The r increased significantly in 1958, stayed the same in 1962, and decreased in 1966. On the other hand, this variable tends to explain the downward trend of the PLN's percentage of the total popular vote since 1953. The party is strongest in cantons whose populations are decreasing.

Industrialization.—Two indicators of industrialization were used in order to present a more accurate overall picture. The first involved the number of workers classified as "industrial" in each population unit of persons gainfully employed. The cantons ranged from a high of 7.3 (San José Central) to a low of 0.5 (Bagaces of Guanacaste). On the surface, this indicator would seem to distinguish typically "industrial" from typically "non-industrial" cantons; there is an inherent weakness, however, because in Costa Rica many types of workers are classified as

TABLE 38

INDUSTRIAL WORKERS

Election		r
Presidential	1953	0.230
Congressional	1953	0.257 (sig.)
Presidential	1958	0.134
Congressional	1958	0.079
Presidential	1962	0.129
Congressional	1962	0.100
Presidential	1966	0.127
Congressional	1966	0.129

industrial whose occupations, by United States standards, are nonindustrial, and at times even agricultural, in nature. Those employed in small soap making, leather tanning, and coffee curing establishments (all are essentially located in rural areas) are lumped together with tool and die makers, machinists, and assembly-line operators. Consequently, the indicator is ambiguous at best. Table 38 illustrates that no pattern of significant relationship exists under this definition.

The second indicator of industrialization measures the per capita consumption of electricity, assuming "modern" or "heavy" industry requires greater amounts of electrical energy than does purely "light" industry. Table 39 demonstrates a significant negative relationship between electrical consumption and PLN support in 1958 and 1962, but none in 1966.

Urban-Rural.—This final variable attempts to demonstrate more clearly the nature of the urban-rural split in Costa Rican politics by correlating the percentage of individuals residing in cities and villages officially considered urban per canton population unit. An inherent difficulty is that the Costa Rican census bureau employs a very liberal definition of the word "urban," and includes many small villages that are quite rural in nature. However, the criteria do separate out the extremely rural localities, and Table 40 does show a significant relationship between the two variables since 1958. Undoubtedly, persons residing in urban areas do not support the PLN to the same extent that their country cousins do.

John Martz, utilizing different statistical techniques to study

TABLE 39

CONSUMPTION OF ELECTRICAL
ENERGY

Election		r
Presidential	1953	−0.012
Congressional	1953	0.060
Presidential	1958	−0.243 (almost sig.)
Congressional	1958	−0.318 (sig.)
Presidential	1962	−0.272 (sig.)
Congressional	1962	−0.310 (sig.)
Presidential	1966	−0.157
Congressional	1966	−0.207

TABLE 40

URBAN RESIDENTS

Election		r
Presidential	1953	−0.218
Congressional	1953	−0.161
Presidential	1958	−0.392 (sig.)
Congressional	1958	−0.456 (sig.)
Presidential	1962	−0.402 (sig.)
Congressional	1962	−0.438 (sig.)
Presidential	1966	−0.325 (sig.)
Congressional	1966	−0.389 (sig.)

the urban-rural voting question, has presented findings which are corroborated by these tables (see note 1 of the present chapter). He demonstrates that the PLN lost the 1966 election because rural voters failed to demonstrate their usual heavy support; his data is substantiated by the downward shift of the r's between 1958 and 1966 in Table 31. Likewise, the lower negative correlations between the same elections in Table 40 give credence to his contention that the party acquired slightly greater urban approval that year. Martz views the loss of rural support as an indicator of a probable future trend. The present

author, however, is inclined to believe that rural alienation can
be explained in terms of PLN candidate Daniel Oduber's public
image. The less sophisticated and more traditional voters of the
countryside were probably more influenced by the opposition's
charges of communism than were the relatively worldwise city
dwellers. It should be noted that the differences between the
legislative r's of the two elections were considerably smaller
than the presidential differences in the tables, implying that

TABLE 41

NATIONAL LIBERATION PARTY SUPPORT COMPARED:
PRESIDENTIAL ELECTION OF 1962

	PLN	PRN	PUN
Land ownership	−0.177	0.168	−0.028
Upper-white-collar	−0.398 (sig.)	0.320 (sig.)	−0.054
Lower-white-collar	−0.391 (sig.)	0.329 (sig.)	0.027
Agricultural	0.409 (sig.)	−0.390 (sig.)	0.054
Blue-collar	−0.356 (sig.)	0.376 (sig.)	−0.113
Service	−0.384 (sig.)	0.346 (sig.)	−0.012
Education	0.242 (al. sig.)	−0.259 (sig.)	0.068
Geog. stability	0.529 (sig.)	−0.520 (sig.)	0.140
Industrial I	0.129	−0.119	0.027
Industrial II	−0.272 (sig.)	0.256 (sig.)	−0.023
Urban-rural	−0.402 (sig.)	0.375 (sig.)	−0.045

voters in general retained their partisan loyalties while casting
their ballots for opposition presidential candidates.

Opposition Parties: A Comparison

Although a consistent pattern of PLN electoral support has
emerged with respect to most of the eleven independent
variables, the lack of extremely high correlation coefficients
might lead the meaning of the pattern to be questioned. To
help buttress the contentions presented thus far, the electoral
support for the two major opposition parties, the National Union
Party (PUN) and the National Republican Party (PRN), were also
correlated to the same independent variables. Only the election
of 1962 serves analytical purposes, however, since that was the
only year in which all three major parties presented candidates
at the presidential and congressional levels. Tables 41 and 42
interestingly demonstrate that in both the presidential and
congressional elections, the coefficient of the PLN vote on each of
the eleven variables was almost a perfect mirror image of the

PRN vote; that is, where the PLN related in a positive fashion, the PRN related negatively and vice versa – *and to almost exactly the same degree.* Thus, further evidence is offered that the two major parties do appeal to different and separate types *of cantons in a regular and consistent fashion.*[23] The lack of significant correlation between Otilio Ulate's PUN and any of the independent variables tends to point up that the National Union Party received its votes randomly and commands no recognizable permanent

TABLE 42

NATIONAL LIBERATION PARTY SUPPORT COMPARED:
CONGRESSIONAL ELECTION OF 1962

	PLN	PRN	PUN
Land ownership	−0.197	0.163	−0.013
Upper-white-collar	−0.425 (sig.)	0.296 (sig.)	0.036
Lower-white-collar	−0.434 (sig.)	0.308 (sig.)	0.009
Agricultural	0.446 (sig.)	−0.376 (sig.)	0.069
Blue-collar	−0.386 (sig.)	0.378 (sig.)	−0.125
Service	−0.422 (sig.)	0.334 (sig.)	−0.037
Education	0.262 (sig.)	−0.254 (sig.)	0.075
Geog. stability	0.563 (sig.)	−0.506 (sig.)	0.150
Industrial I	0.100	−0.135	0.027
Industrial II	−0.310 (sig.)	0.245 (sig.)	−0.036
Urban-rural	−0.438 (sig.)	0.358 (sig.)	−0.058

support base. The differences between the structural support bases of the parties becomes even more apparent when the 1962 cantonal vote of each is correlated to its rivals. Table 43 demonstrates a very high negative relationship between the PLN and PRN and no significant relationship between the PLN and the PUN. These data also tend to support the suggestion made in footnote fifteen of the present chapter that the PRN (with PUN support) should be considered the "other" party in Costa Rican politics.

As a sidenote, the 1962 election also provides an interesting opportunity to analyze extreme leftist support relative to the

23. It might be argued that the data presented here are invalid because, in a two-party election, correlations for one party with any given set of independent variables would have to be mirror images of the other party's correlations. The fact remains, however, that the presidential election of 1962 was *not* a two-party election because the PUN supported a separate candidate and received 13.5 per cent of the total valid vote. Although the percentage is not high, it could have changed the mirror image effects noticeably if the PLN and PRN did not appeal to different types of voters in a systematic fashion.

major parties, for in that year a fourth party, the temporary and small Popular Democratic Alliance (PADP), offered both presidential and congressional candidates. Although not openly Communist, the PADP did attract many sympathizers and was supported by leaders of the illegal Popular Vanguard Party. The data below proved quite conclusively that cantons which supported the PADP also supported the Republican Party and did not support the National Liberation Party. The PUN again shows no

TABLE 43

INTERPARTY CORRELATION, 1962

	PRN		PUN	
	Pres.	Cong.	Pres.	Cong.
PLN presidential	−0.839	−0.818	−0.063	−0.018
PLN congressional	−0.822	−0.802	−0.057	−0.042

TABLE 44

PADP SUPPORT AND OTHER POLITICAL PARTIES, 1962

	PLN		PRN		PUN	
	Pres.	Cong.	Pres.	Cong.	Pres.	Cong.
PADP presidential	−0.621	−0.600	0.545	0.500	−0.111	−0.102
PADP congressional	−0.663	−0.654	0.583	0.527	−0.099	−0.105

significant relationship. These data tend to support the PLN claim, strongly denied by the Calderonistas, that voting patterns established during the 1943–48 period of PRN-PVP coalition still remain, and cantons containing the greatest numbers of the nation's pro-Communists also support Republican candidates.

General Conclusions

None of the eleven variables fully supports the central hypothesis *that the National Liberation Party's base of popular support is undergoing a gradual but consistent shift.* Although an impressive change can be noted between the 1953 and 1958 r's for most of the variables, there is little change thereafter. Also, a not quite significant but relatively strong negative correlation exists between the increase in 1953–58 voter turnout and the PLN's vote in 1958, implying that the opposition made a determined effort to mobilize potential followers in 1958. Therefore, the hypothesis is rejected in favor of an alternative that better fits the results.

In 1953 José Figueres, as the undaunted hero of the 1948 War of National Liberation, appealed to a wide stratum of the population. His personal charisma cut across class, occupational, and business lines. Also, lack of a well-defined opposition that year helped insure the "randomness" of his support. By 1958, however, the PLN structure had solidified, no strong charismatic candidate was leading the party ticket, and individuals voted more according to social and economic interests. At the same time the opposition effort in 1958 helped divide the electorate into two camps. These factors explain the lack of correlations between the PLN's 1953 percentage and most of the eleven independent variables as well as the significant correlations found after 1958.

Explaining the continued downward shift in the r's of Table 25 after 1962 is much more difficult. It can only be suggested that once the PLN base was established, it slowly continued to lose some of its local support. Also, the drastic increase in voter turnout after the 1959 compulsory voting law probably aided the opposition and this upset the overall pattern a little. The PRN's cantonal percentages in 1962, correlated with voter increase between 1958 and 1962, produced an r of 0.197, while the PLN's vote produced a -0.101. Although these coefficients are *not* statistically significant at the 0.05 level, they do indicate the probable trend. The data supporting these suggestions are admittedly weak, but on the other hand the decrease in the r's in Table 25 from election to election is not great either. It is only when the entire sixteen-year period is viewed as a whole that the shift becomes impressive. Therefore, slight but consistent changes each electoral period — changes too delicate to be measured by the rather crude yardsticks presently available — could account for the overall shift.

Aside from the question of support shift, the data in this chapter seem to indicate that since 1958 the National Liberation Party has possessed a regular support base from which it draws most of its votes. Therefore, LaPalombara and Weiner's fourth criterion of the modern party, that it must in some manner seek popular support, is true *ipso facto*. Generally, the more rural, uncommercial, unindustrial cantons with little population turnover tend to vote PLN.[24] Since those areas have been steadily losing individuals to the urban centers with greater economic opportunity, the party has steadily decreased its percentage of the total national electorate since 1953. Also, it appears that as rural persons move to the cities they fail to take along their partisan loyalties. Unless the PLN substantially improves its electoral position in the cities, it may continue to lose support as it has in the past.

24. Daniel Goldrich has presented data which appear to contradict these conclusions. Interviews with well-to-do Costa Rican schoolchildren enrolled in high prestige Catholic schools in San José indicated that, of the 79 per cent who maintained strong partisan identifications, 43 per cent favored the PLN, 21 per cent the PUN, and 14 per cent the PRN. He concludes: "Thus, over time, the PLN appears to be recruiting a much larger proportion of the establishment, which suggests the possibility that the national political integration problems of the future may be generated within that party, as the range of interests it aggregates expands, rather than between it and its older and weaker competitors." See *Sons of the Establishment: Elite Youth in Panama and Costa Rica*, pp. 50–51.

7. Liberacionista Ideology and Program
Historical Precedents, 1940-1951

MODERN PARTIES with modernizing missions have an additional characteristic, a reasonably well-defined program or ideology based on transforming the total society. Such parties seek pluralism, integration, mass mobilization, and higher economic standards. This chapter and the one that follows trace the development of PLN political, economic, and social thought from the early 1940's to the present and measure the party against this fifth criterion.

The years prior to 1951 are important since they represent a period of basic policy formation. After that date the party was a major political force with a congealed and solidified political, economic, and social doctrine. Therefore, it is important to understand the manner in which that doctrine was established and from what sources it was derived. The two groups which in 1945 formed the Social Democratic Party, National Liberation's lineal ancestor, each brought with them certain ideas and programs, although the Center for the Study of National Problems, because of its unique existence as a study group, was much more influential in the final formation of liberacionista thought. Acción Demócrata, which had been a branch of the Cortesista

118

Party until 1944, never developed a deep or far-ranging program of its own and had satisfied itself by denouncing the Calderón government, personalistic political parties, and undemocratic practices in general.[1] The Center, on the other hand, had maintained study committees and lecture courses for five years and consequently developed a relatively coherent and unified doctrine which was carried over to the Social Democratic Party after 1945. For this reason the Center will be examined more closely than its contemporary. Unless specifically noted otherwise, the following analysis of the Center should be considered applicable to both groups.[2]

Political Program

In general, the centrista political program was a moderate one, heavily influenced from the beginning by the Peruvian Apristas. Articles and reports written by centrista members during the early years contain numerous references to Haya de la Torre, his movement, and his ideology.[3] The small group of students and young professionals who composed the Center for the Study of National Problems felt their chief responsibility was to educate the public towards what its members conceived to be democratic goals, for only education and culture could "elevate the man and citizen to the awareness of his responsibilities, to the understanding and enjoyment of liberty; to active cooperation in the perfection of the social forms of life."[4] Such emphasis was put upon "education" and "culture" because centristas felt that only by understanding the history, geography, demography,

1. The little that has been written about AD program and thought can be found in three issues of *Acción Demócrata* (Mar. 4, 11, and 18 of 1944) and a small printed pamphlet *Declaración de Principios y Reglamento Interno*. Also see "Acción Demócrata y el capitalismo nacional," *Acción Demócrata* (Mar. 18, 1944), p. 2.

2. In 1943 the Center for the Study of National Problems published the results of a survey of political and economic attitudes in which members of AD had been asked to participate. The study is most interesting since it demonstrates the similarity of beliefs between members of the two groups. See *Ideario costarricense*.

3. A report by Luis F. Morúa for the Center's Commission on Social and Economic Affairs entitled "El A.P.R.A., modelo de los movimientos políticos–sociales en indoamérica," spells out in detail the Center's reliance on Aprista concepts. Archives of the Center for the Study of National Problems, San José. Also indicative of the same attitude is Rodrigo N. Madrigal, "Haya de la Torre y el Aprismo," *Surco*, no. 50 (Oct., 1944), p. 11.

4. "De la declaración de principios y de los estatutos del Centro," *Surco*, no. 13 (June, 1941), p. 16.

and political and social systems of Costa Rica could any real understanding of national problems be attained.[5] In other words, it was a basic point *that all nations had particular and unique patterns and that no fixed social dogma could necessarily apply to all nations.* This sentiment, a major proposition of Aprismo, was echoed by Rodrigo Madrigal in a study-committee report concerning Costa Rican cooperatives:

> The problem at the beginning was completely a Costa Rican one, and for the most part had to be resolved by Costa Rican methods. Our situation cannot be resolved with difficult theories of foreign manufacturing, but with an intensive national organization. We believe, like Haya de la Torre, that "it is imperative to recognize the relation of Space and Time in order to appreciate these phases or degrees of evolution." And we admit that since the realities have been different, the problems themselves as well as their solutions have had to be different also. In summary we should envelop our economic, social and political problem in its own environment and not seek European formulas and doctrines as one would acquire a new piece of machinery or a new suit. We should not backslide into the demagogic mumble-jumble of our communists and creole fascists that has thus far produced only "common places of the highest vulgarity."[6]

In other words, what might have solved the problems of one nation might only complicate and aggravate the problems of another. For example, federalism may have served as a means of gaining consensus between the varying social areas of the United States, but to Costa Rica, with its history of unity and centralism, federation could only have served a disunifying

5. This point was made over and over again by Professor Carlos Monge. He lamented the fact that Costa Ricans really knew very little of their national heritage and consequently could hardly be expected to understand their nation's problems. "There is no nation in the world more anti-historical than Costa Rica. None of us knows anything of or have any interest in the past. We can see this, for example, in our [educational] programs; national history only occupies one year—the first—of the five of secondary education. It is proverbial that our children know more of Bonaparte, Caesar, Ramses II, and Hammurabi than of the virtues of our own people." "El Liberalismo en Costa Rica," *Surco*, no. 43 (Jan., 1944), pp. 8–9. The same theme in somewhat different form is expressed in Eugenio V. Rodriguez, "Hacia una verdadera justicia social," Archives of the Center for the Study of National Problems, San José.

6. Rodrigo Madrigal, "El Centro ante el cooperativismo," Archives of the Center for the Study of National Problems, San José.

function. Again, Marxism with its concepts of class warfare was also rejected by centristas, who felt the goal in Costa Rica should be the stimulation of new sources of national wealth, not the redistribution of what small amount there already was. "The idea of a political movement founded on the radical theory of the struggle of the proletariat against the bourgeois, for example, is totally alien to Costa Rican necessities and possibilities. . . ."[7]

The Center's view of society necessitated a pluralistic polity with organized and competing political groups dedicated to goals and principles.

> Our concept of the State differs from that which our Father-land has traditionally maintained as a community. We do not believe that the State should be part of the patrimony of a governing party nor of the President in power. The State should be for all (for the governors as well as the governed; for friends as well as enemies of those who govern). The State should never be a cheap political instrument and less, much less, an electoral instrument.[8]

One of the worst evils of Costa Rican history, centristas believed, was the total lack of strong, viable, ideologically oriented political parties. "Our group," declared an official statement of centrista program, "is the organized manifestation of the new generation. . . . We are the vanguard of the young people who are ready to terminate the corrupted, cheap, political practices and are ready to put order into the economic and social life. . . ."[9] The personalist "parties" which had governed the nation since independence were deemed to be completely inept when it came to solving grand-scale social problems. That point of view was summarized quite well by Gerardo Fernandez in 1943: "We firmly believe that personalist parties imply a grave danger for the people, who have waived their right to establish the type and composition of public policy they desire for the Govern-

7. Rodrigo Facio, *Estudio sobre la economía costarricense*, p. 164. Especially indicative of this attitude is an article by Haya de la Torre, "Frente único, y no lucha clasista," *Acción Demócrata* (May 12, 1945), p. 3. The related problem of underproduction and underexploitation of valuable resources was also fundamental to centrista economic thought.

8. "Acción del Centro: Algunos de nuestros conceptos políticos," *Diario de Costa Rica* (July 28, 1943).

9. "Programa del 'Centro para el Estudio de Problemas Nacionales,'" Archives of the Center for the Study of National Problems, San José.

122 Liberación Nacional in Costa Rica

ment, for their Government; for that reason we have not approved any of those parties and we strongly criticize them."[10] A similar statement on the disintegrating effects of personalist politics was enunciated by Professor Monge: "We note that since that faraway era [the electoral campaign of 1889] politics have been characterized by ideological nonsense, audacity of attacks, and vulgarity and morbid passion of the campaign directors."[11] Not only had political parties been temporary personalistic aggregations in the past, but they had continued in that capacity into the mid-twentieth century. Centrista thought maintained that no political group in the nation, with the exception of the Communist Party, was making the slightest attempt to modernize itself into an ideological force. Alberto F. Cañas characterized the methods used by the contenders in the 1944 campaign in the following manner:

> The propaganda raised by the parties in the current electoral struggle is similar in its general lines to that delivered in other epochs of Costa Rican history. Again we have heard and read uncouth statements, vulgarities, offenses, and lies; again the morale of the citizen has been lowered; again there have occurred insults as well as personal or familial allusions. In spite of the inconveniences that such a method of seeking followers creates for civic morale, in spite of the little advantage gained, the writers and orators of the parties, who are dedicated to the most irresponsible of tasks, have continued their work through articles and radio tranmissions, with words and phrases so base, so obscene, that conscientious persons have become alarmed. The directors of those groups have formulated programs, have been presented as persons of a new political lineage, have affirmed that their activities are motivated toward the analysis of ideas, and have assured that for Costa Rica begins "HER SECOND INDEPENDENCE" or have incited the citizenry to "SAVE YOUR FATHERLAND, VOTE FOR SO AND SO." They have also promised that the candidates and deputies will be chosen in popular conventions, that the peasants will have fertile land, that the cost of [living will be lowered] from one moment to the next, and many other things. Nevertheless, Costa Rica waits as in limbo for these things.[12]

10. Gerardo Fernandez, "En defensa de nuestra democracia," *Surco*, no. 38 (Aug., 1943), p. 3.

11. Carlos Monge, "Vieja y nueva política," *Surco*, no. 44 (Feb., 1944), p. 8.

12. Alberto F. Cañas, "Propaganda politiquero y propaganda política," *Surco*,

This lengthy description of the Center's attitude towards personalist Costa Rican parties has been deemed necessary because of its fundamental nature to overall centrista political ideology. Not only must parties be stable and ideological but responsible, responsible both to their members and to the Costa Rican citizenry as a whole. This point was hammered over and over again by centrista writers. For example, as early as 1941 Gonzalo Facio wrote: "To bring about these social phenomena that we have considered as fundamental elements of democratic climate, it is necessary that the principle of Government, as an authentic delegation of the popular will, should be applied. In that order the existence of one organism is decreed absolutely essential, *The Doctrinaire Political Party.*"[13]

It would not only be necessary to establish such parties; citizens would have to take an active role once they were established.

> The citizen of a democracy must assert unto himself the duty of analyzing, of criticizing, and of judging public functions and public servants. This is without doubt the pillar which supports dynamic life in democracies, as opposed to totalitarian regimes. It is this duty, not citizens' rights, that creates a regime of public opinion which then allows political life within a republican system of government. Consequently, this duty is the base which supports the existence of organic, doctrinaire, permanent political parties.[14]

Moreover, the Republic of Costa Rica was thought to have arrived at the point of maturity where such political parties could be established.[15]

Before concluding this outline of the Center's political program, a few words must be said concerning the group's attitude

---

no. 43 (Jan., 1944), p. 1.

13. Gonzalo Facio, "Necesidad de los partidos políticos doctrinales en la democracia," *Surco*, no. 13 (June, 1941), p. 3. Also see Facio, "Ni la Constitución ni los Fines, ni la trayectoria de los tres partidos en lucha podían nunca satifacer el Anhelo que nos Une," *Diario de Costa Rica* (July 15, 1943), p. 1, and "El Partido Doctrinario contra la política personalista," *Acción Demócrata* (Apr. 7, 1945), p. 3.

14. Rafael Alberto Zúñiga, "Prepárese la ciudadanía costarricense para vivir en el régimen de la opinión pública al traves de la voluntád política de los partidos ideológicos," *Surco*, no. 29 (Nov., 1942), p. 1.

15. Alberto F. Cañas, "El país está maduro para la formación de un partido ideológico democrático," *Surco*, no. 42 (Dec., 1943), p.1.

towards communism. It was unalterably opposed to all forms of totalitarian systems. For that reason the centristas opposed both international fascism[16] as well as international communism. The concept of responsible partisan struggle again played an important role: it was felt that true liberty could only be obtained through a clash of differing political viewpoints. The concept of a single authority, exercising complete political authority, was indeed alien to Center members. As a result, the Center opposed the Partido Vanguardia Popular, Costa Rica's Communist Party, at every turn and particularly denounced the PVP's growing influence in the government of President Calderón:

> After the "group of minstrels" [i.e., the followers of Calderón] came the "shock troops" or the armed organizations of the Communist party, who broke with the national tradition of pacifism by introducing into the national political activity the opening of heads with blackjacks and did it all in the name of the Labor Code, the United Nations, democracy, the Act of Social Guarantees, and the Atlantic Charter. And the Government, in exchange for their support, conceded absolute immunity to the Communists and their shock troops. . . . [17]

Economic Program

The economic program of the groups which preceded the National Liberation Party was similar to their political program in that it was also heavily influenced by the Aprista movement and was quite evolutionary and mild. "We do not believe nor pretend — because we are not dreamers — that [our programs] can be realized in a violent manner. On the contrary, we believe it should be a slow and cautious undertaking. . . ."[18] Interspersed with this moderation was a strong element of economic nationalism, most

16. In 1941 the Center joined eight other Costa Rican youth organizations to form the United National Front of Opposition to Fascism.

17. Special issue devoted to a criticism of the administration of R. A. Calderón Guardia, "La Política Social," *Surco*, no. 47 (May–June, 1944), p. 51. Also see "Ante el pacto Republicano Nacional-Vanguardia Popular," *Surco*, no. 40 (Oct., 1943), pp. 1–6; "Emplasamos al Partido Vanguardia Popular en Defensa de Nuestra Democracia Política," *Diario de Costa Rica* (Aug. 6, 1943), p. 1; and "La ciudadanía sabe bien que el Centro no tiene ningún nexo con el gobierno ni con el comunismo," *Diario de Costa Rica* (Aug. 20, 1943), p. 1.

18. Zúñiga, "Hacia una política económica definida," *Surco*, no. 25 (July, 1942), p. 8.

of which was directed toward the foreign owners of certain national monopolies. "Foreign capital—the real motor of our growth—forced, in relation with the necessities of the world market, a monoculture economy of coffee, provoking enormous steps backwards as well as paralyzing the development of production...."[19]

Property was deemed to have a social function. Classical liberalism with its emphasis on entrepreneurial rights was rejected because it offered no guarantee of economic security to the nation as a whole. Rodrigo Facio attempted to describe a new "middle position" that would permit private property and fulfill society's economic goals at the same time: "In recent years a species of neo-liberalism has been sought, which is today a transactional formula between economic liberalism and state socialism. The problem of possibly conciliating, in a Democracy, the principles of political liberty with social and economic security has been tackled.[20]

Centristas favored a greater degree of state regulation, planning, and government supported industrialization. This type of mixed economy has always remained a pillar of liberacionista thought. As early as 1943 José Figueres, still in exile, defended the middle position, advocating "a mixed economy, *of private property with state regulation,* of private businesses and public institutions...."[21] Although the middle position between laissez faire capitalism and social statism might yield the most beneficial results, the Costa Rican body politic had always been denied such a program: "In reality the quack politicians, those that have defended the great capitalistic interests, are similar to the communists who are interested only in the class struggle of the industrial proletariat. Between both groups the people, that broad group for whom democracy was created, are nothing but sheep that are conducted at certain times to the electoral slaughterhouse."[22] More specific reforms included a nonpolitical civil service,[23] a workable social security system, an enforced minimum

19. Facio, *Estudio sobre la economía,* p. 159.
20. Cited by Constantino C. Lascaris, *Desarrollo de las ideas filosóficas en Costa Rica,* pp. 324–25.
21. José Figueres, *Palabras Gastadas,* pp. 19–20.
22. "El Centro piensa: Campaña de cultura cívica democrática," *La Hora* (July 20, 1943).
23. During the 1940's the spoils system operated in Costa Rica much as it had in the United States during the nineteenth century, and government employees

wage law, government protection of the rights of workers,[24] and a more realistic tax system which would include a great deal of administrative reform.

Earlier in this chapter it was noted that centrista thought rejected the Communist notion of class warfare because it was felt that economic prosperity would be best accomplished by creating new sources of wealth, not simply redistributing the little already existing.[25] Costa Rica, centristas argued, was under-exploited, and the only answer to the problem would be the stimulation of unproductive resources. "Our problem is different: in Costa Rica, all national wealth has not been exploited enough."[26] To help solve this problem cooperatives were founded and encouraged, and this area provided an opportunity for genuine activity. For the most part National Liberation's predecessors had little opportunity to implement their policies before 1948. Therefore, most proposals remained just that, proposals and goals. In most cases the Center was content to describe what *should* be done, and *how* it was to be done. Such, however, was not the case with cooperatives. Not only did their creation remain one of the Center's theoretical goals, but direct action was taken towards their implementation. "Above all we mean that our conviction regarding the excellence of the cooperative ideal is absolute, and that, in consonance with our ideology, we have always advocated, within the social and economic possibilities of the nation, the formation of cooperatives, even before they appeared in contemporary social legislation."[27] They sought to introduce coopera-

---

were expected to engage actively in partisan affairs. "In the first place," stated a centrista editorial, "we should make a clear difference between what is meant by political activity and what is involved within the concept of 'examination of the conduct of the public powers.' In Costa Rica the concepts have been confused and this has brought with it a tremendous demoralization to the state servant." "Acción del Centro: Reformar electorales; prohibición de actividades políticas a los empleados públicos," *Diario de Costa Rica* (May 14, 1943). Also see "Desarrollo del programa: Objectivo inmediato de la política económica social," *Acción Demócrata* (Jan. 19, 1946).

24. See "Complementos necesarios de las garantías sociales," *Diario de Costa Rica* (Apr. 28, 1943).

25. See above, p. 121.

26. "El máximo problema de Costa Rica es el de que toda su riqueza aún no ha sido explotada," *Diario de Costa Rica* (Nov. 30, 1943), p. 9. Also see "Dice el Centro: Mientras nuestra producción sea insuficiente, poco se avanzará con imponer precios oficiales a las cosas," *La Hora* (Mar. 30, 1943).

27. Zúñiga, "La importancia del sistema cooperativo en Costa Rica," *Surco*, no. 40 (Oct., 1943), p. 12.

tives which would not only organize the buying and selling functions of their members, but would provide certain services as well. Adult education, group insurance, cheap electricity and water, local transportation, and recreational facilities were only a few of the tasks such cooperatives would undertake. It was strongly emphasized that all decisions pertaining to cooperative activities should be made through the democratic process. A General Assembly was to be the "supreme authority" of each cooperative with an administrative Junta Directiva responsible to it. Officers and directors were to be elected for a fixed period and could be removed by the General Assembly.[28]

Centrista writers attempted to connect their work with earlier European cooperative experiments. Emilio Valverde described the English Rochdale cooperative of 1844 and its work in establishing the Cooperative Wholesale Society in 1864, the German Raiffersen and Schulze-Delizsch groups, the work of Charles Gide, and other Scandinavian and Swiss successes.[29] Vicente Lombardo Toledano attempted to liken the work of the Center in this area to the ejido system in his native Mexico.[30] By the end of 1945, twenty cooperatives of various types had been organized throughout the Republic of Costa Rica.[31] Private companies such as the Bank of Costa Rica, the Electric Company, and unions such as the Federation of Graphic Arts had founded credit and mutual aid societies for their employees and members. Campesino organizations like the Unión de Tres Rios had been established in order to purchase consumer goods cheaply. The Center maintained contact with most of these organizations and had been instrumental in founding several of them. Part of the Center's activities included the creation of a Department of Cooperatives within the National Bank and the "cooperativization" of all confiscated enemy property.[32]

28. See Zúñiga, "Principios administrativos de las cooperativas," *Surco*, no. 31 (Jan., 1943), p. 21.

29. Emilio Valverde, "Origen y desarrollo de las cooperativas," *Surco*, no. 31 (Jan., 1943), p. 21.

30. See Vicente Lombardo Toledano, "Organizaciones de planificación cooperativas de consumo por tierras de América: Vicente Lombardo Toledano habla para *Surco*," *Surco*, no. 31 (Jan., 1943), pp. 5–7.

31. For interesting data on the formation of cooperatives in Costa Rica, see Eugenio Rodriguez Vega, *Apuntes para una sociología Costarricense*, pp. 51–56; and Madrigal, "El centro ante el cooperativismo."

32. See "Acción del Centro: Por la cooperativización de la propiedad enemiga," *Diario de Costa Rica* (July 7, 1943).

The Social Democratic Party

The political and economic program developed by the Center for the Study of National Problems during the five-year period 1940–45 was adopted almost in toto by the Social Democratic Party (PSD). This was so for two major reasons. First, Acción Demócrata had never really worked out a definite ideology or program of its own during the three years of its existence; and, second, members of AD shared many of the same attitudes as members of the Center. In general, social progress was to be accomplished only by constitutional means; and violence, in any form, was rejected as a means of political action.[33] All governments were to be based on the will of the people determined by free elections with universal suffrage. All religious faiths were to enjoy equal status. Free and public education was to be absolutely guaranteed to all children. Small farms and small industries were to be financially encouraged by the government and an overall national development plan was to be made. Foreign capital was to be protected so long as it did not interfere with the economic well-being of the nation. National finances were to be reorganized and a professional civil service with a high degree of technical knowledge was to be founded. Public health, hygiene, and sanitation were to be involved in the overall development plan. Cooperatives and unions of all types were to be established and encouraged. Finally, Costa Rica was to maintain relations only with nations whose governments expressed the free will of their people; all other nations were to be shunned.[34]

However, the social thought of the PSD differed in one important aspect from that of the Center. It has been stated that the Center had rejected *all* European and foreign ideologies in favor of an Aprista-inspired reliance on domestic answers to domestic problems. During the first several years of organization the PSD followed this approach and did not affiliate itself with European-inspired international organizations. Instead, it maintained friendly relations with like-minded political parties throughout

33. It should be remembered that the party came to power in 1948 by waging a successful "War of National Liberation."
34. Complete statements of the PSD program can be found in "Programa ideológico del Partido Social Demócrata presentado al Registro Electoral," *El Social Demócrata* (Oct. 2, 1948); and Partido Social Demócrata, *Resúmen del Programa del Gobierno del Partido Social Demócrata.* Also see "Haga conocer a todas nuestros 12 postulados," *Surco*, no. 53 (June, 1945), pp. 18–19.

Central and South America.[35] Letters written on October 11, 1947 to Alberto Carnevalli of Venezuela's Democratic Action Party, Dr. Jorge Eliécer Gaitán of Colombia's Liberal Party, and Haya de la Torre reveal the PSD's deep commitment to cooperate with other Latin American "Popular parties" in the solution of mutual problems.[36] By 1950, however, the PSD was widely endorsing the program of the international socialist movement as well as supporting social democratic and socialist parties across the world. This shift in attitude is all the more noteworthy since the name "Social Democratic Party" was adopted in 1945 only as a compromise, and it will be remembered that the PSD had almost become the Social Republican Party.[37] Later issues of *El Social Demócrata* continued to glorify European socialist parties.[38]

By 1951, the year the National Liberation Party was founded, the precedents for a fairly coherent and inclusive political and economic program had been established. Those precedents drew upon a variety of sources including the revisionist doctrines of European socialism and the domestic oriented approach of the Latin American Apristas, tempered by the pragmatism of the New Deal and twentieth-century regulatory liberalism. The democratic process was emphasized above all, and a higher standard of living was deemed most important in order to make the process work.

35. For example, an article in *Acción Demócrata* on Apr. 7, 1945, entitled "El Partido Social Demócrata le ofrece su cooperación al Presidente Arévalo de Guatemala," testified to the friendly relations between the PSD and Guatemala's Revolutionary Party.
36. Archives of the Social Democratic Party, San José.
37. See above.
38. Especially significant are "Mensaje de la Conferencia Internacional Socialista" (May 13, 1950); and "Ideas y figuras del socialismo democrático" (May 27, 1950).

8. Liberacionista Ideology and Program "Official" Party Doctrine, 1951-1970

W HEN the National Liberation Party was founded in 1951, the roots for a reasonably coherent ideology had already been established, yet the realities of practical politics have destroyed much of the clarity and cohesion over the decades. In the previous chapter it was noted that during the early years of formation partisan writers identified their movement with Aprista-type indigenous parties throughout the hemisphere and rejected European-originated doctrine outright. It has also been noted that by the late 1940's that identification had been weakened and replaced by ideas of the international socialist movement. "Officially" this is still the case because older PLN leftists (the now middle-aged youths of the generation of 1948) have been the most prolific spokesmen of party doctrine. However, the "official line" should be studied with extreme caution for three reasons. First, conservatism in the PLN is very strong. Conservatives, who tend to be a bit older and wealthier than the "older leftists," are usually less ideological in nature and seldom publish their news. They unenthusiastically support the official line in principle and ignore it in practice; hence their real views cannot be ascertained. Even in candid interviews they seldom attack the party's left-leaning rhetoric, although they are often

130

eager to slur the persons responsible for that rhetoric. One gets the impression that they are most concerned with the power aspects of politics: patronage, prestige, and government contracts. Second, younger liberacionistas, most of whom tend to affiliate with the Juventud (JL), have been influenced in recent years by the New Left concepts of American and Western European youths. Their favorites are Regis Debray, Albert Camus, Herbert Marcuse, the Students for a Democratic Society, and the radical student movements of France and Germany; some of the more extreme elements openly cherish Ché Guevara, Ho Chi Minh, and Mao Tse-tung. They, like the conservatives, seldom speak for the party as a whole; they cannot gain access to the PLN press and do not have adequate funds to publish their beliefs. Besides, the JL structure has been controlled by Juventud moderates who have chosen to refrain from embarrassing the regular party. The Declaration of the Patio de Agua, described elsewhere, provides insights into the attitudes and goals of the PLN left. Third, those who publish the official statements of the party, although usually associated with the left, are always the most pragmatic of their colleagues and cautiously seek to avoid dogmatic stands on controversial issues.

Consequently, a moderate and "respectable" brand of socialism should be considered the National Liberation Party's central concept. Former presidential candidate Daniel Oduber has made this point with remarkable clarity. According to Oduber, the PLN assumes a position which "in Europe and Latin America is known by the name of 'social democratic' and in the United States goes by the name of 'liberal.'"

> This position, in many aspects, is a healthy reaction against the cruel excesses of the so-called manchesterian liberalism practiced in the nineteenth century and brought ... prosperity to a few nations and, at the same time, misery to workers. Those excesses also produced Marxism.
>
> In synthesis, our political opinion is that the modern State can liquidate the excesses mentioned and economically and socially emancipate the dispossessed masses without sacrificing the basic democratic liberties ultimately known as "Human Rights." *That is to say that one can eliminate the inequalities and injustices that economic liberalism brought without forsaking the postulates of political liberalism.* [Italics added for emphasis.]

In Latin America this has been the position of José Batlle y Ordóñez, Victor Raul Haya de la Torre, Pedro Aguirre Cerda, José Figueres, Rómulo Betancourt, and other notable statesmen. . . .

In the United States the "New Deal" of President Roosevelt . . . represented the crystalization of this tendency and has been continued by presidents Truman, Kennedy and Johnson. It has also been doctrinarily expounded in continuous form by the historian Arthur Schlesinger, Senator Eugene McCarthy, . . . and . . . Hubert Humphrey. . . .

The North American liberals and the Latin American and European social democrats are concerned with the above-mentioned problems. . . .[1]

The excerpts are highly indicative of official PLN thought, which is all the more moderate (or nebulous) because the central term, "socialism," has a very soft connotation in the small Central American republic. "In Costa Rica," states José Figueres, "the word socialism simply conveys images of the good life, of honest elections, of economic well being. By no means does it bring to mind ideas of class struggle as it does in the United States or parts of Europe."[2] Liberacionista spokesmen often substitute the term "Democratic Left" when speaking of socialism or liberalism.

This attitude, that all parties of the "Democratic Left" belong to one large, happy, international family, is also reflected in the PLN's relations with foreign parties and international political organizations. A founding member of the League of Latin American Popular Parties, which also includes Venezuela's Democratic Action Party, Peru's Aprista Party, and Bolivia's National Revolutionary Movement, National Liberation has also supported the Inter-American Association for Democracy and Freedom, which has brought together many liberal Latin American and North American politicians and intellectuals, as well as founding a training school for young but promising leaders of the Demo-

1. Daniel Oduber, *De Donde Venimos*, pp. 10–16. The reader should keep in mind that no attempt is made in this chapter to evaluate PLN ideology and program, except from the standpoint of LaPalombara and Weiner's fifth criterion. The following pages are a condensation of what PLN leaders say their goals are and in no way reflect the author's views. Whether or not the leaders involved really believe their pronouncements is deemed immaterial to the study.
2. Interview with José Figueres (Mar. 29, 1966).

cratic Left. In addition, it has been able to maintain working ties
with other hemispheric groups, most notably the Social Christian
and Christian Democratic parties. Finally, the PLN has been a
member of the Socialist International since 1964 and currently
enjoys growing friendships with the British Labour Party and
the German Social Democratic Party. These relations tend to
give top PLN leaders local stature as international political
figures.

Even warmer (and unquestionably more advantageous at
times) are the relations between the PLN and the liberal wing of
the United States Democratic Party. As early as the mid-1940's
an editorial published by the Social Democratic Party testified
to the fact that even at that time future National Liberation leaders were in sympathy with Roosevelt's party:

> The Democratic Party, the party that in 1932 brought
> Franklin Roosevelt to power, has been amply defeated in
> the [1946 Congressional] elections. The Republican Party,
> whose last president was Herbert Hoover, has gained a
> great triumph. For us Latin Americans the triumph of the
> Republicans is truly alarming inasmuch as it might signify
> a change from Roosevelt's Good Neighbor Policy. We see
> in the Republican Party of the United States a narrow view
> of the problems of the world; we see in its triumph a real
> danger that we will return to the age of Dollar Diplomacy
> in which our relations with the United States will be based
> upon Marine landings.[3]

"We identify ourselves completely with the type of people who
compose such organizations in your country as the Americans
for Democratic Action," Figueres told this writer, "we feel we
must ally with some important [American] groups and the liberal
Democrats are the most logical choice." When asked if his party's
reliance on a single North American political group might not be
disadvantageous at times, Figueres replied: "Indeed it might.
We have already experienced considerable embarassment in the
past from the Republican Eisenhower administration because
of our policy of cooperating with North American liberals."[4]

Much of the PLN's official ideology and program is an uncontroversial appeal to civic virtue and social reform. Man is
both individual and social, both spiritual and material. He pos-

3. *Acción Demócrata* (Nov. 23, 1946), p. 4.
4. Interview (Mar. 29, 1966).

sesses certain inherent rights which under no circumstances may be denied him. These rights are "the indispensable instrument for the realization of his destiny and for his cooperation in completing the destiny of the community."[5] Liberty includes not only traditional civil and political rights but also possession of the essentials of life. Without adequate food, clothing, and shelter no person is deemed to be truly free. In addition to liberty, the common good is essential to both man and society—it is roughly the production and just distribution of an adequate supply of man's necessities. Democracy is defined as "a political system inspired by the respect of human dignity within which the government is a conscious delegation of the sovereign bodies of people, and they exercise it maintaining respect for minority groups."[6] Both private property and labor are deemed to serve social functions, and individuals are to be guaranteed honest and remunerated work at all times. The reader should be aware that Costa Rican politicians of most persuasions and partisan groups have long endorsed similar goals and proposals.

The Political and Social Thought of José Figueres

Because the PLN has been so overwhelmingly dominated by the personality of José Figueres, his political and social thought will be used as a means of describing official party doctrine; Figueres has consistently been the party's chief spokesman and it is only fitting that he be given credit for general PLN attitudes.

Employing techniques of analogy and symbolism, Figueres has successfully brought his ideas to public attention through his ability to reduce broad political ideas into everyday terms: "To navigate in a boat without direction, to travel in a herd of senseless sheep, to live in a country governed by a despot are not the acts of rational beings. Our eyes were given us in order to see, our reason in order to understand, and our will in order to guide our lives. Whosoever covers our vision, obscures our understanding, or cuts our will robs us of something more valuable and damages our individuality more than he who steals our wallet or burns our house."[7]

Attempting to illustrate his belief in three basic concepts— economic development, social welfare, and the rule of law—

5. Partido Liberación Nacional, "Carta Fundamental," p. 3.
6. Ibid., p. 4.
7. "Democracia," *Acción Demócrata* (June 17, 1944), p. 3.

Figueres again used analogy to emphasize his point by likening each of the three concepts to a San José skyscraper:

> I believe in the value of symbols. Today in the capital of the Republic there are three buildings of impressive symbolism. Three multi-storeyed structures which in our modest view seem like skyscrapers and which represent three aspects of our country's progress: the Central Bank (development), the Department of Social Security (welfare) and the Law Courts (the rule of law). The Pharaohs used the national purse for building the Pyramids to deify themselves; the Romans for building coliseums for bloody gladiatorial games; in the age of faith people reached up to Heaven through the tall spires of the Gothic Churches; the aristocracy of all ages lived in palaces; the merchants of the nineteenth century used granite and marble for the opulent offices of their private banks; military regimes built barracks; and civilisation now reaching out into space creates buildings of more than a hundred storeys on the island of Manhattan. Meanwhile, in the heart of the Continent of America, in a little country whose anthem is dedicated to manual labour, three monuments in modern concrete and steel are being built — monuments to the three aspirations of the age: economic development, social welfare and the rule of law.[8]

Above all, Figueres wants to be known as a democrat as well as a socialist. Democracy, he defines, as "a society in which each individual has a clear knowledge of what the group does; it is a collaboration of all in the management of things that pertain to all; a collaboration that manifests itself in an ordered and rational form...."[9] His belief in the democratic process was evidenced in 1958 when his party lost a popular election after he had been president for four and a half years. Although there was some doubt that he would turn over the reins of government to his opponent, he did so with grace. "I consider our defeat a contribution to democracy. It is not customary for the party in power to lose an election."[10] An outer form of democratic "window dressing" is not enough to qualify a particular state

8. José Figueres Ferrer, "My Political Testament," *Socialist International Information*, pp. 63–65.
9. Figueres, *Palabras Gastadas*, p. 11.
10. *The New York Times* (Feb. 6, 1958).

as a democracy. There must be an overall respect for legal institutions, for the customs of society, and for the rule of law. "A country is not democratic by the fact that it celebrates periodic elections, or because it is given that name by the persons who govern it. If there is no spirit of political community and of participation in responsibilities; if the suffrage, the free expression of thought, or the majesty of tribunals of justice are not respected religiously, there is no democracy. Democracy is not demagogy."[11] Another fundamental of democracy is absolute respect for the rights and dignity of the individual:

> Fortunate is the citizen of a nation where justice rules; where the respect for human dignity is fundamental in all relations; where the beneficial restrictions, as guiding measures, do not come from an arbitrary individual, astute or wise, nor from a small group, but from the will of those that form it, maintain it, and defend it, conforming to the tacit agreement of the social aggregate; he has obtained what he expects from his union with other men: he has transcended himself. Because his physical forces, his economic potential, and above all the faith in his dignity given by the God of Creation, have multiplied as many times as the group of individuals. And that man is free.[12]

Figueres conceives democracy in such a manner, a manner representing the classical liberal tradition. He adds nothing new that had not been covered by eighteenth- and nineteenth-century political thinkers, but neither does he attempt to distort the meaning of those early thinkers. He has never construed democracy to mean "tutelary democracy," "developing democracy," or other distortions which have been used by certain very undemocratic political leaders in recent decades.

Socialism, the second concept fundamental to Figueres' thought, has previously been described as something tantamount to social justice and economic progress. It is of a Western variety which permits moderation and encourages, in turn, a type of mixed society. It is noteworthy that Figueres has never really clarified the role of the state in the type of society he desires. Obviously, the state is a necessary instrument, but the extent to

11. Figueres, *Palabras Gastadas*, p. 12.
12. Figueres, *Palabras Gastadas*, p. 34 (1943 edition) as trans. by John F. Wolff in "José Figueres of Costa Rica: His Theory and Politics as a Model for Latin American Development and Security," p. 73.

which it should be used has not been determined. Actually, socialism, like democracy, has usually been described in general and laudatory terms. "Socialism," Figueres believes, "is the aspiration toward an economic order in which each gives the maximum of his capacities in the organized production of the necessities of life in exchange for a standard of living high enough to permit accumulated wealth with the daily production of his labor."[13] Economic planning is necessary but should be "based on a combination of public institutions and private enterprises."[14] Consequently, it appears that the state is only to engage in economic matters when absolutely necessary. It is to be responsible for overall economic planning and administration. State ownership of productive resources is not an end in itself but merely a means to an end— only when private capital is unable to provide a desired service. Private property is deemed to have a "social purpose" and is to be held inviolable so long as that purpose is fulfilled. Only "socially unproductive" property may be seized by the state and put to better use. However, a few industries and services, because of their fundamental value to the society, should not remain in private hands. One such industry was banking; it was deemed to have an impact on the economy so great that society (i.e., the state) had to control it directly. Following this principle, the entire Costa Rican banking system was nationalized by the Founding Junta in 1948.[15]

Adhering to Western socialist tradition, welfare has played a very predominant role in Figueres' social thought. Twentieth-century ideas and practices must be put to work if Costa Rica is to progress: "It follows that we must make a fresh examination of the position of our country in conjunction with other nations and with history. And we must begin the new life by following not only the great ideologies of the Eighteenth Century but those that have been transforming the world since the mid-Nineteenth Century, since the industrial revolution and the two world

13. Figueres, *Palabras Gastadas*, p. 20.
14. Figueres, *Inaugural Address* (Nov. 8, 1953), p. 4.
15. For two National Liberation Party defenses of the nationalization of Costa Rica's banks, see *Nacionalización bancaria en Costa Rica*; and Rufino Gil Pacheco, *La nacionalización bancaria*. Opponents of the National Liberation Party often charge that the banks were nationalized in order to allow members of Figueres' revolutionary junta access to low-interest loans. Another criticism has centered around alleged administrative inefficiency in the government-owned system.

wars.''[16] Respect for individual dignity and worth is not enough; such concepts are meaningless without the guarantee of adequate living standards. Only if the individual possesses the necessities of life may he successfully contribute to the general betterment. Wages, not laws of supply and demand, should determine prices. Workers should be guaranteed salaries commensurate with living requirements, and market fluctuations should not be allowed to jeopardize family income. Likewise, prices of international commodities should be set according to wages, and international commissions should supervise minimum wage standards:

> Large areas are devoted almost exclusively (because of climate and history) to the production of international commodities. This production is a way of life. It determines, directly and indirectly, the standards of living of a large part of the less developed world. Yet, little attention has been paid in development programs to the need for fair, *uniform* minimum wages.
>
> The world will not develop until the prices of international commodities, and the wages paid for their production, are regulated internationally, product by product; until a *development price* is established for the exports of underdeveloped areas; until *uniform minimum wages* prevent undercompetition among the poor nations.[17]

In conclusion to this description of Figueres' political and social thought, a few words must be included concerning his attitude towards communism and Communist penetration in Latin America. Like other founders of the National Liberation Party, he has always been opposed to the Marxist doctrine of class struggle as well as totalitarian techniques practiced in some Communist nations. Regarding the former, Figueres believes class warfare is both destructive and avoidable. If it is to exist at all it should exist in a constructive manner:

> Class struggle? So be it. Let it be the constructive ideas of the employers and the honest workers, against those dictated by short range egoism of the agitator or the bourgeois.

16. Quoted in Hugo Navarro Bolandi, *José Figueres en la evolución de Costa Rica*, p. 19.

17. Figueres, "Wages," quoted with permission from the author. Many of Figueres' early attitudes on social welfare and planning can be found in *Doctrina social y jornales crecientes.*

Class Struggle? So be it. Let it be the struggle of those classes which plan the hymn of labor . . . against the classes of parasites, both above and below. Social revolution? So be it. Let it be the revolution against inefficient methods of work, which are not good enough to cook bread enough for all, and against the retrograde methods which are useful to no one. But let the struggle of ideas, the struggle of classes, and the social revolution be contests among rational human beings, in a democratic battlefield, where each brain is a cannon, where each enemy is a friend. *And above all let it never be a fratricidal struggle among the elements necessary to production. . . .* [Italics added.][18]

Figueres' position on the second point, Communist totalitarian techniques, is best illustrated by his unfriendly attitude toward the regime of Fidel Castro.[19] Although Figueres had given weapons, supplies, and other aid to Castro during the early days of the Cuban Revolution, he was one of the first to denounce Havana when he perceived threats to civil liberties. The former United States ambassador to Costa Rica, Whiting Willauer, testified that as early as March, 1959, Figueres told him Castro's government "is a Communist matter, or if it is not already it is about to be."[20] Figueres has been one of the foremost Latin American liberal leaders in the struggle against Cuban communism since that time. He believes there are two exterior social revolutions at work in contemporary Latin America, both "intimately affect the life of our country and that of neighboring countries."

On one side is the Cuban Revolution as part of the Communist Revolution in Latin America.

On the other side the Alliance for Progress is a symbol of the Western answer to the threat of Russia and China. This social program coincides with the thought of the Latin American popular parties, National Liberation of Costa Rica among them.

Our America is today an empty lake that will inexorably

18. Figueres, *Palabras Gastadas*, p. 27 (1943 edition), as trans. by Wolff, p. 72.
19. See Figueres, "Liberación Nacional ante la Revolución Cubana."
20. U.S. Senate, Committee on the Judiciary, "Communist Threat to the United States through the Caribbean," *Hearings Before the Subcommittee to Investigate the Administration of the Internal Security Act and Other Internal Security Laws of the Committee on the Judiciary*, Part 13, 87th Cong. (Mar.–July, 1961).

be filled in the next few years by one of the two current movements, the communist revolution or the social democratic one. The present situation cannot prevail.

... National Liberation is with the Alliance for Progress. There is more: National Liberation believes to have contributed, together with other Latin American parties, to marking out that road, to formulating its program, and keeping alive the faith in a free and prosperous American Hemisphere united as equals in friendship.[21]

Such is the overall political and social thought of José Figueres — a combination of classical liberal values emphasizing faith in the democratic process, the rule of law, and respect for the individual, together with Western socialist beliefs in the social use of private property and active state participation in economic development. Running throughout are strong strains of pragmatism, moderation, and optimism. It is, in short, quite typical of liberacionista thought in general.

Specific National Liberation Program

The economic goal of the PLN has been to raise overall Costa Rican productivity and income by as great a margin as possible without nationalizing private property. Economic progress in the past had always been hampered by the lack of a good system of transportation. Lacking facilities to deliver cash crops to markets, huge areas have remained unexploited. The party has proposed the extension and modernization of the nation's system of roads and highways, the enlargement of the ports of Puntarenas and Limón, and the unification of the two national railway systems under a single authority. The PLN has also encouraged the use of government loans and subsidies to develop remote areas. Government controlled research into diseases of coffee, cacao, bananas, tobacco, cotton, and cattle has been established during the two PLN administrations, and technical assistance of other types has been made available directly to the producer. Above all, stable international prices have been urged. Figueres and other party spokesmen have repeatedly stated that substantial price guarantees might do more to develop agricultural Latin American nations than international loans, grants, and subsidies.

21. Excerpts from Figueres, *Dos Revoluciones: La Revolución Cubana y la Alianza para el Progreso*, pp. 7–27.

Specific PLN economic goals have included more than improvement of the national agricultural system. Diversification has been encouraged and new industries have been aided in order to protect the nation from the effects of overimportation and over-reliance on fluctuating agricultural prices. National Liberation Party economists have argued that industrialization should come first in areas affecting Costa Rican products. Therefore, roasting plants for coffee and processing plants for other agricultural goods have been given first priority. Attempts have been made to coordinate the training of technicians and specialists for the new plants and new technological schools have been instituted. A PLN-sponsored Law of Industrial Promotion has encouraged foreign investment by offering certain tax privileges and governmental assistance. Finally, the promotion of mining, tourism, and commerce has also been deemed necessary to national well-being, and agencies to deal with these endeavors have been established or expanded.[22]

Since 1965 National Liberation economists have attempted to capture public imagination with a program called the Plan of Universal Capitalization. According to this scheme, employable persons will be encouraged to purchase shares in new industries and allowed to take part in the decision-making process of the corporations. In time workers would own a major portion of national productive resources and directly benefit from their labor. Extremes of wealth and poverty would hopefully be diminished. In certain senses, the Plan represents continuation of the cooperative program begun by the Center for the Study of National Problems in the early 1940's.[23]

Since Costa Rica is limited by relatively little native capital, National Liberation theorists plan to use their Plan of Universal Capitalization in conjuction with autonomous institutions. Such organizations, owned in part by the government, are viewed as a method of avoiding economic statism while developing native capital potential. In the early 1970's only certain service institu-

22. For various PLN economic programs, see Partido Liberación Nacional, *Programa económico*; Partido Liberación Nacional, *Plataforma Política*; Partido Liberación Nacional, Secretaria de Capacitación, *Nuestra economía*; Juventud Liberacionista de Costa Rica, *Un programa económico específico para Costa Rica*; and Partido Liberación Nacional, *Nuestro Programa de Trabajo, 1966–1970.*

23. See Partido Liberación Nacional, *Nuestro Programa*, pp. 19–20; and *La Nación* (Jan. 29, 1966), p. 12.

tions such as banks, the light and power company, the national housing development, and agricultural cooperatives fit in this category, but PLN leaders maintain that future administrations will make further use of this type of administrative procedure.

Closely related to the problem of industrialization is the problem of labor, for the party has never made much headway in converting industrial-urban workers to its banner. The importance of the workers vote to the party has been attested by Luis Alberto Monge:

> The only logical and natural bases upon which to build the stability and growth of our Party are the following, listed in order of importance:
> (a) The rural middle classes (small and medium-sized landholders).
> (b) Urban and rural salaried workers (industrial workers and day laborers).
> (c) White collar workers, the lower-middle class and mid-middle class (servants of the State and its institutions, commercial employees, artisans, grocers, bookkeepers, travel agents, etc.).[24]

Social reforms of the early 1940's have always been upheld and in certain cases strengthened by the PLN. National Liberation Party members insist that many of the laws enacted at that time were never enforced until the Founding Junta of the Second Republic came to power in 1948, and coverage of social security programs has been broadened by both the 1953–58 Figueres administration and the 1962–66 Orlich administration. The party points to the fact that more persons are now covered, expenditures are greater, and the types of services are more diverse. Furthermore, the National Institute of Housing and Urbanism (INVU), a government owned autonomous agency founded during the Figueres administration, has built and financed inexpensive but attractive homes for thousands of low income wage earners who would otherwise be unable to own their homes.[25]

Besides its support for industrial welfare programs, the PLN

24. Memorandum from Luis Alberto Monge to members of the National Executive Committee (Sept. 3, 1963), quoted with permission from the author.
25. See Partido Liberación Nacional, *El trabajador y el Partido Liberación Nacional.* A short review of PLN activities in the field of workers benefits will be found in Francisco Orlich, *Plataforma política para la administración Orlich, 1958–1962;* and Daniel Oduber, "Discurso de la campaña electoral."

has always supported democratic labor unions in their struggle for improved wage scales and working conditions. "They [persons opposed to the formation of unions] do not realize," stated Daniel Oduber, "that if free and responsible democratic unions did not exist, they would be the first to be swept away by the disorganized masses, goaded on by Communist sermons."[26] As early as 1942 the Center for the Study of National Problems declared that it "would strongly support an organized movement of Costa Rican workers dedicated to democratic principles."[27]

Although there had been several unsuccessful attempts to establish trade unions in the early twentieth century, only the Communists had managed to organize Costa Rican workers before 1943. Father Benjamín Nuñez, a priest strongly influenced by Roosevelt's New Deal while studying at the Catholic University in Washington, D.C., was asked by his bishop to found a movement based upon the various papal encyclicals dealing with social welfare. Nuñez agreed, but only on four conditions: first, that the movement would in no way be used for religious proselytism; second, that no confessional restrictions be put on members; third, that the movement would be in no way dependent on ecclesiastical authority; and, fourth, that the movement would not be called "Catholic." These conditions were met, and the new movement was officially named the Confederación Costarricense de Trabajo Rerum Novarum (CCTRN), or simply Rerum Novarum. It will be remembered that in 1943 the Communists, who controlled the Confederación de Trabajadores de Costa Rica (CTCR), were in coalition with the Calderón government and were, therefore, able to bring strong political pressures against the new group of Father Nuñez. Similarly, the opposition parties, particularly the Partido Cortesista, strongly desired to increase their support among the working classes and gave economic support to the CCTRN. In this manner, Rerum Novarum became affiliated with the opposition during the 1945–48 period of intensive political hostility. When the revolution broke out in 1948 Nuñez and his labor leaders joined don Pepe in the mountains and took an active part on the front lines. As a result, Nuñez was appointed Minister of Labor in the Founding

26. Daniel Oduber, "Mensaje a los trabajadores," pp. 4–5.
27. Centro para el Estudio de Problemas Nacionales, "El Centro para el Estudio de Problemas Nacionales y el trabajador costarricense," Archives of the Center for the Study of National Problems, San José.

Junta of the Second Republic and from that position obtained a court decision dissolving the Communist Confederation of Workers in 1949.[28] Later Rerum Novarum leaders served PLN governments, usually in the Ministry of Labor or related organizations. Ironically, some of the more energetic of them such as Father Nuñez, Luis Alberto Monge, Armando Arauz, Alfonso Carro, Otto Fallas, and Jorge Rossi gave so much time to the party that the union, left to lesser men, became less effective.

Between 1951 and the mid-1960's the PLN supported, and retained semiformal ties with, Rerum Novarum. However, relations between the two began to erode during the 1962–66 Orlich administration. Although the Ministry of Labor under Alfonso Carro supported labor's goals, the Ministry of Security was accused of persecuting labor leaders (including some from the Rerum Novarum) under the guise of investigating communism. The union finally appealed to the International Labor Organization in 1965 after a complete break with the party. The following year, shortly after Oduber's defeat, a major reorganization merged the debilitated labor group with certain independent unions to form the Costa Rican Confederation of Democratic Workers. However, ties between the new union and the PLN's currently alienated left wing have remained close; union leaders enthusiastically supported Oduber's candidacy, and later they were instrumental in framing the Patio de Agua Declaration.

Finally, the improvement of free public education has long been another PLN goal. "I believe that in the halls and classrooms of our schools prime importance should be given to everything concerning Costa Rican civic education . . ." wrote Daniel Oduber.[29] In 1951 the Fundamental Charter of the PLN recognized the need for a national educational system which could fulfill the practical needs of an industrial age, and the 1953–58 Figueres administration enacted the Fundamental Law of Education, which provided funds to fulfill many of the educational provisions of the 1949 Constitution.

As a result, the Ministry of Education was strengthened and

28. Most of the above information was obtained during an interview with Father Benjamín Nuñez (Apr. 29, 1966). Useful in analyzing the Rerum Novarum during its early years is his book *ABC del sindicalismo*; a contemporary description of the country's labor movement can be found in Joseph J. McGovern, "The Costa Rican Labor Movement: A Study in Political Unionism," *Public and International Affairs*, pp. 88–116.

29. Daniel Oduber, *La educación, la mujer y la política.*

provided with technical departments corresponding to the various subject matters taught. Separate administrative agencies were created for primary, secondary, normal, and vocational schools; and administrators appointed to head the new agencies were given practical experience in the United States, Puerto Rico, and Chile before assuming their positions. Finally, a cultural program was instituted whereby many Costa Rican university professors might take paid leaves to pursue their specialities in United States or Puerto Rican graduate schools. Consequently Costa Rica has improved itself in this area to the point where it now attracts foreign students from other Central American nations, students that had formerly gone to Mexico, the United States, or Europe for their educations.[30]

General Conclusions

The National Liberation Party fits the criterion of the "Modernizing Party," that a reasonably well-defined ideology based on the concept of social change be present. However, extreme differences of opinion and open hostility between its various wings have tended to denegate the importance of doctrine. There are, in fact, several National Liberation parties, each with its own beliefs, goals, attitudes, and solutions. Yet, a central thread of thought, a thread that has been labelled the "official line," has run throughout; though moderate and quite nebulous in many areas, it is most certainly "modernizing" enough for the criterion, especially when the total lack of ideological content in earlier partisan groups is considered.

Beginning as an Aprista-styled Latin American popular party, the PLN slowly changed its ideological point of view and today identifies with European social democratic parties and the liberal wing of the United States Democratic Party. It has always believed that true social change is best accomplished by relatively slow deliberative measures, not unplanned immediate revolution. National Liberation has really added nothing new to contemporary political ideology, but it has successfully applied many attitudes of the classical liberals, the European revisionists, the twentieth-century regulatory liberals, the Latin American Apristas, and to some extent the Christian Democrats.

30. See Partido Liberación Nacional, "Programa de Educación."

9. Development of Modern Political Parties in Transitional Societies

T HE NUMBER of alphabetical political groups that have emerged for brief periods during the past two generations in Latin America alone must surely be in excess of a thousand. Adding the totals for all African plus Middle and Far Eastern nations would produce a staggering number. Why is it that so many would-be parties become organized, exist for a few months or years, and then disappear, while a few others become viable and permanent institutions? This study has attempted to shed light on the answer to that question by examining a single case, Costa Rica's National Liberation Party. It has been emphasized that the PLN fulfills all (but possibly one) of the criteria and can properly be considered a modern party with a modernizing mission in a transitional society. The following section summarizes the major conclusions regarding those criteria, and relevant general patterns of party establishment are then considered.

The National Liberation Party and the Five Criteria of the Modern Party

First, the PLN has continuity. Originated in the early 1940's as a protest movement of upper-middle-class youths, it has

146

grown and become institutionalized. Although the original
founders are still alive and still actively engaged in the party's
activities, it seems quite probable that the PLN will continue, in
some form, after they have departed. (Yet, it must be re-empha-
sized that National Liberation is undergoing very bitter interfac-
tional disputes as this is written in early 1970, and it is conceivable
that a large segment of younger, left-leaning leaders will permanently leave, thus weakening the party's stability even further.)
The students of the Center for the Study of National Problems
merged with the young politicians of the Cortesista Party in
1945 to found the Social Democratic Party (PSD), one of Costa
Rica's first partisan organizations with permanent (although not
very widespread) political structure, intraparty democracy, and
a reasonably coherent program or ideology.

Because the PSD was too small to compete on its own during
the 1945–48 period, it joined the coalition of parties opposed to
the Calderón-Picado-Mora government. That coalition was
composed of three schools of thought which cut across party
lines to some extent: the first would have collaborated with the
government, the second favored continued opposition but not to
the point of violence, and the third proposed armed revolution.
José Figueres led the last school and was supported by a
majority of PSD members. Together Figueres and the PSD waged
a successful "War of National Liberation" in the spring of 1948
and assumed control of the Costa Rican government until late
1949. Figueres became a national hero overnight. Beginning in
1951 the Generation of '48 utilized his popularity by organizing
a nationwide political party based on the PSD structure. That
party, the present PLN, has become the single largest partisan
organization in Costa Rica and has held executive power twice
as this is written. Thus, the first hypothesis can be tentatively
accepted, although it must be admitted that the forthcoming
decade might easily witness the collapse of this apparently
viable structure.

Second, the PLN is organized at the local levels; the local
leaders communicate regularly, although indirectly, with
national leaders. Between 1951 and 1953, leaders of the Generation of '48 organized committees in about four-fifths of the
nation's districts and nearly all cantons. Electoral victory in 1953
assured greater local support and by 1958 the party was completely organized at all levels. In contrast to the national leaders,

leaders recruited to fill the party's local ranks tended to be from lower-middle-class or working-class families, less educated, less politicized, less ideologically oriented, and more authoritarian. They were, in other words, representative of *el pueblo*, "common folks." One important characteristic distinguished them from the masses, however; they were much more energetic and upwardly mobile.[1] Although many of the local leaders came from agricultural or industrial working-class homes, very few maintained such occupations themselves, even at the very lowest levels of the PLN hierarchy.

Although regular factions do exist at the national level, no evidence was discovered that such factions are a usual phenomenon at the local levels, or that local leaders support any of the national factions in any systematic manner. This may be due to the fact that local units "go to sleep" shortly after each quadrennial election and do not "awaken" until six or seven months before the next. It is believed that if elections were held more often, greater local infighting would occur.

Third and fourth, the PLN actively seeks control of the Costa Rican government at all levels and also seeks popular support. Since the two criteria are so intimately connected in a democratic system, where political power is obtained at the ballot box, they were considered jointly. Since 1953 the PLN has won two of the four presidential elections, an absolute majority of legislative seats during the entire period, plus approximately 50 per cent of all local municipal council seats in all elections. At the present time it is campaigning in an enthusiastic manner against determined opposition.

Since 1958 the PLN has been supported by cantons which are more rural and agricultural and whose population is static and unchanging. It cannot count on those cantons that are more industrial, commercial, or dynamic in the sense of population growth. These bases of support could change drastically, however. Beginning in 1964 a group of PLN national leaders associated with the party's "left wing" or "progressive wing" led by Luis Alberto Monge, José Luis Molina, and others has

1. Of the gainfully employed Costa Rican population, 79.7 per cent maintain some type of working-class occupation, whereas only 12.6 per cent of the post-1951 PLN recruits in the sample hold such jobs. Likewise, 89.1 per cent of the population over the age of twenty-five are limited to primary school educations against 13.8 per cent of the recruited leaders.

endeavored to strengthen the party's unfavorable image among urban workers. There is limited evidence that their work met with minor success in 1966.

In 1953 the PLN obtained its votes randomly and was not supported by regular types of voters. This was probably due to the nature of the candidate. José Figueres, as the hero of the 1948 War of National Liberation, maintained a charismatic following which cut across class, occupational, and regional lines. Besides, the PLN had only recently been organized as a mass movement and permanent party loyalties were not yet solidified. Beginning in 1958, voters apparently tended to vote for the party rather than the candidate, and consistent patterns have emerged since that date.

The percentage of the electorate that has supported the party has been decreasing regularly since 1953. If this trend continues, and if the PRN and PUN can maintain their electoral alliance or completely merge into a single party, the PLN might well become the permanent minority party in future decades. At present, however, loyalties of the electorate remain closely divided between the PLN and its opposition.

Fifth, the PLN fulfills the criterion of a special type of modern party, the "modernizing" party, by sponsoring a reasonably coherent political ideology aimed at transforming the total society. Originally based on the political thought of Haya de la Torre and the Latin American Aprista movement, the PLN has changed its emphasis over the years and is now very much in line with the European social democrats and North American liberals. Its leaders maintain close and friendly relations with several European political organizations, particularly the British Labour Party, the German Social Democratic Party, and the Socialist Parties of Denmark and Sweden, with leaders of the liberal wing of the United States Democratic Party, and with certain Latin American reformist parties, including the Venezuelan Democratic Action Party, the Peruvian Aprista Party, and the Dominican Revolutionary Party.

Theories of Party Establishment

LaPalombara and Weiner have summarized three sets of theories relating to the explanation of political party organization. The first involves institutional factors dealing with parliamentary coalitions. Here it is argued that like-minded legislators begin sitting together, caucusing separately, and eventually form a primitive partisan structure which ultimately establishes local units. Although such a pattern was undoubtedly the norm in certain nations, including France, Britain, and the United States, this explanation had little to do with the Costa Rican experience and shall not be considered further. The second set of theories involves the overall process of modernization and hypothesizes that political parties somehow "come about" when the nation reaches a sociological level of sufficient complexity to necessitate such elaborate structures. The third set might be termed the "crisis theories." Transitional societies are faced with certain problems that require immediate attention for which the traditional structures are unprepared. The latter two relate to the historical process in Costa Rica and shall be considered separately and then together.

Modernization and Party Origin

The forces of modernization which contributed to the establishment of the PLN were similar to those in most nations undergoing the transition from a traditional, rural, family-oriented society to one that is more modern, urban, and pluralistic. The political party is:

> . . . a creature of modern and modernizing political systems. Whether one thinks of Anglo-American democracies or totalitarian systems such as the Soviet Union, Fascist Italy, and Nazi Germany; emergent African states in their earliest years of independent evolution or Latin American republics that have hobbled along for over a century, a mammoth ex-colonial area such as India groping toward democracy or an equally mammoth Communist power such as China seeking to mobilize a population through totalitarian methods, the political party in one form or another is omnipresent.[2]

Certainly the dynamics of political life are not identical in any two nations, let alone that all-inclusive thing called the Underdeveloped World. Costa Rica, for example, has maintained a tradition of responsible government and respect for fair play unmatched in all but a few comparable nations. Relative lack of religious hostilities, militarism, and highly personalist rule over

2. Joseph LaPalombara and Myron Weiner, "The Origin and Development of Political Parties," in *Political Parties and Political Development*, pp. 7–21.

extended periods also make it a bit unique, but all these factors have been present in Costa Rica to some degree and the overall process is not vastly different from that in Nigeria, Cambodia, Pakistan, and elsewhere. Although Costa Rica might have been a bit better off in terms of certain political problems, it fits within the general pattern of such nations undergoing a shift in the ways of political life. Parties, interest groups, professional associations, and similar organizations were almost unknown in Costa Rica before the late 1930's. Normal duties of such groups were generally fulfilled by other structures – the family, the Church, the military. Due to Costa Rica's rather unique tradition of secularism and civilian rule, the last two never became as important in this respect as they have in most traditional societies, so the burden fell by default to the former. During the nineteenth and well into the twentieth centuries large extended clans encompassing dozens, even hundreds, of cousins, uncles, aunts, and nephews served as vehicles for getting things done. Whether a new oxcart trail had to be built to transport agricultural products, a position on the public payroll was desired, or a government contract was sought, one normally consulted a relative. The uncle who was the *gamonal* of the local village, the nephew who served in the Ministry of Agriculture, the distant cousin (for some reason always by marriage) who became Vice-Minister of Government all served as recruiter, block captain, ward heeler, national committeeman, and potential presidential candidate of an invisible and unorganized political party. Coalitions of such extended families made or broke governmental leaders. To be seriously considered for a very high position one almost had to be of the *familias principales* that wielded money, power, and support.

Such a family-centered polity was in no way dysfunctional. Given the simplicity of the society and the leisurely tempo of life in this tropical and comfortable climate, things worked quite well. By the 1930's, however, internal forces began to make such a primitive type of organization obsolete. Newer, more organized structures were demanded. The national population, never very large in the nineteenth century,[3] was rapidly approaching a million; no longer could the family adequately serve in its previous capacity, no longer could everyone "know"

3. According to the 1864, 1883, and 1892 censuses there were 120,499, 182,073, and 243,205, respectively.

everyone else in anything even remotely approaching a literal sense. The number of persons simply became too large.

The coffee industry, established in Costa Rica on a large scale shortly after the American Civil War, initiated the modernization process by bringing into the nation monetary wealth unknown in earlier days.[4] By the 1930's, after three generations, that wealth had become institutionalized and affected the transition in two major ways. First, it created a set of class problems by supporting a new privileged group based not on family and heritage as before, but on money. Although the influence of the *familias principales* broke down and class ties lessened in a social sense, the newer group sought privileges undreamed of in earlier and simpler days. Consequently, the gulf between the haves and the have-nots widened. As money became more important, family ties became less so, and financially successful members of the important clans broke contact with their less wealthy relatives, who in turn helped form the nucleus of a new upper-middle class.

The second effect of the coffee industry complemented the first. The new wealth created a need for increased commercial activity, and urban areas grew enormously in the space of a few decades. The cities of the Meseta Central, particularly the national capital of San José, never more than sleepy villages before, attracted individuals from rural areas by offering greater economic opportunities. New types of employees were needed to staff the offices, factories, and banks; so a lower-middle class was established. Over a period of time this element lost contact with relatives still in the country and class ties tended to break down even more. At the same time the new commercial element tended to merge with less successful members of the old important families, and the "invisible" political parties based on family and family coalitions continued to erode. As a result, large and increasingly active sectors of the population were without political voice. By the late 1930's and early 1940's a new type of political vehicle was clearly needed.

National Crisis and Party Origin

The second set of theories hypothesizes that crises in the political, social, or economic systems of a nation stimulate party

---

4. For a detailed analysis of the social effects of the coffee industry, see Rodrigo Facio, *Estudio sobre la economía costarricense*.

organization and even dictate what patterns that organization will take.[5] "New institutions are created that persist long after the factors which precipitated their creation have disappeared; and memories are established in the minds of those who participated or perceived the events that have subsequent effects on political behavior."[6] The Calderón government alienated wide segments of the population by breaking traditional patterns of ruling. Reliance on the nation's Communists further discouraged many individuals, and a crisis situation arose with a sizeable percentage of the politically active citizenry refusing to support the authorities between 1942 and 1948. Out of this six years' crisis emerged a number of new political groups—groups with structural sophistication vastly superior to any previously known. The Center for the Study of National Problems underwent a transmutation from a small student discussion club to a dynamic and enthusiastic (although small) corps of partisan leaders. Acción Demócrata, originally only a subsidiary structure of the highly personalist Democratic or Cortesista Party, adopted a separate identity of its own and after merging with the Center in 1945 developed an organizational framework which eventually surpassed the parent party. At the same time publisher Otilio Ulate founded the National Union Party, an institution that continued after the political life of its *jefe* had expired. Although the PUN never attained the complexity, size, or organizational sophistication of the PLN, it has served as a base for the political activity of the nation's more conservative elements.

Charismatic Leaders and Political Party Origin

Although social science literature from Weber[7] through Lasswell[8] and Morton[9] is abundant with studies of the strong and popular political leader and his effect on the polity, few authors have considered the possibility that permanent political

5. By "political crises" LaPalombara and Weiner do not refer to the usual concept (plagues, revolutions, wars, depressions, and so forth). Although these "parametric changes" may precipitate political crises, the term is reserved for breakdowns of legitimacy, integration, and participation.

6. LaPalombara and Weiner, *Political Parties*, p. 14.

7. Max Weber, "Politik als Beruf," *Gesammelte Politische Schriften*, pp. 396–450.

8. Harold D. Lasswell, *Psychopathology and Politics;* and *Power and Personality.*

9. Ward M. Morton, *Castro as Charismatic Leader.*

parties may be due, at least in part, to the dynamism of a single individual. This is partially due to the fact that most serious students of party formation view highly personalist politics as representative of traditional, premodern political systems, yet is it not possible that parties beginning as personalist machines might outlive the leader and later become modern, nonpersonalist, viable institutions? Mexico's Institutional Revolutionary Party (PRI) is today one of the least personalistic of all Latin American parties, yet in its early days it was dominated by a caudillo, Plutarco Calles. Likewise, the Peruvian Aprista Party will probably perpetuate itself long after its charismatic founder and caudillo, Victor Raul Haya de la Torre, passes from the political scene. Professor Dauer has explained the passing of the United States Federalist Party in economic and social terms;[10] the Federalists, supported by the more wealthy elements of society, were unable to appeal to the increasingly active small farmers and urban workers, hence the party collapsed. While this thesis has considerable merit, is it not likely that the Federalist Party would have continued, or perhaps even grown, had it had a strong and dynamic leader with great popular appeal? Although John Adams possessed many political talents, it can hardly be argued that he fulfilled the criteria of the charismatic leader.

The effects of the popular hero on party establishment are nowhere more apparent than in the National Liberation Party. The ability of José Figueres to secure the loyalties of wide segments of the population undoubtedly contributed to PLN successes during the formative years. Many persons identifying as liberacionistas in the 1960's were Figueristas in the late 1940's and early 1950's. The small group of political architects that composed the original leadership cadre could never have hoped to put together a large force without the image of don Pepe as a selling point. Chapter 6 indicated that Figueres' appeal was so strong that it cut across social and economic lines and attracted voters from all walks of life, hence no significant correlation could be found between the 1953 vote and ten of the eleven independent variables. After 1958, with Figueres no longer in the political limelight, the party "settled down" and consistent patterns of support were established.

10. Manning J. Dauer, *The Adams Federalists.*

Before terminating this general discussion of the effects of charismatic leaders on partisan organization, it must be noted that Costa Rica's second strongest party, the National Republican Party, was established in almost identical fashion. Little more than the personalist vehicle of Rafael Calderón Guardia during the 1942–48 period, it has become a stable and permanent institution in recent years. Although Calderón still exerts some influence over the rank and file as an elder statesman, his activities are extremely limited, and the party is now run by younger leaders of a different generation. If the 1965 merger with the National Union Party survives the test of time, this group will become even stronger and less personalistic. Younger leaders of both parties seem to prefer joint action, but animosities dating from the 1940's plus basic ideological differences might prevent total union.

Final Conclusions

Why did the National Liberation Party become a viable and permanent component of the national political system while other groups in Costa Rica and similar groups in similar nations have failed? Essentially, there are three reasons, all of which are important in explaining the phenomenon. First, the times were right. Costa Rica had reached the point in its social and economic development where old political methods could no longer suffice. New groups and sectors were becoming increasingly important and institutions had to be formed to enable them to participate in national politics. Also, a crisis period was at hand and a swift solution was demanded.[11] Second, a small group of determined, intelligent youths was available to serve as the leadership cadre of such a new political organization. Having previously worked together as members of a nonpolitical cultural association, they had acquired organizational experience which could later be channeled into partisan activities. Third, the charismatic personality of José Figueres attracted mass support in the early years by appealing to voters from all regions, classes, and occupations.

It is highly questionable that the PLN could have attained its present status without any one of the three factors. If the times

11. Of course, it may be argued that a nation undergoing such a swift transition is in a state of perpetual crisis due to the lack of stability in the system. The author would subscribe to this view.

had not yet been right, family ties would have kept the nucleus of leaders from cooperating together for common ends. Without the nucleus of leaders, Figueres' personal following would have disbanded after his presidential administration. Without Figueres the small PSD would not have attracted mass support and probably would have remained a small group of upper-middle-class intellectuals.

It appears that these factors have been connected to the establishment of political parties in Latin America and perhaps the rest of the world. When one or more have been absent, modern permanent parties do not seem to have materialized. Traditionally, legislatures in Latin America have been weak, so no Franco-Anglo-American style parliamentary-originated party has yet emerged, although certain "government parties" such as Mexico's Institutional Revolutionary Party or El Salvador's National Conciliation Party might be viewed as Latin American equivalents. In almost all cases the parties that seem to have "made it" developed in the opposition, more or less outside normal governmental channels. This was true not only of the National Liberation Party but of others as well, notably Venezuela's Democratic Action Party, Peru's Aprista Party, and Chile's Christian Democratic Party. In all four cases the three factors were present. The times were right, a well-disciplined cadre of leaders energetically organized the party, and a strong, charismatic leader solidified mass support. Liberacionistas had don Pepe, the Adecos Rómulo Betancourt, the Apristas Victor Raul Haya de la Torre, and the Christian Democrats Eduardo Frei. At the other extreme, nations such as Argentina with over a hundred fragmented political groups or Ecuador and Haiti with practically no organized partisan activity at all have lacked one or more of the necessary ingredients. Further investigations are needed to test these hypotheses.

As a case study in the establishment, development, and internal processes of a single political party in a single nation, it is hoped that the conclusions of this work may be generalized to include similar parties in similar nations and ultimately contribute to the understanding of party behavior.

10. The Sample of National Liberation Party Leaders

E ACH INTERVIEW took approximately one hour and fifteen minutes and followed a highly structured questionnaire schedule containing both open-ended and closed-ended items. Almost all respondents were extremely cooperative and very few difficulties were encountered either in obtaining appointments or in conducting the interviews. Most leaders, especially those with a purely local base of operation, felt delighted to be offered an opportunity to present their views to an outsider and nearly all expressed their thoughts with depth, openness, and candor. On only four occasions did the author feel true expressions were being changed or colored in any way. The leaders appeared to have definite notions about the way things were (or should be) and were not about to miss a chance to air those notions.

The 103 respondents were selected in the following manner. Fifty-seven of the nation's sixty-eight cantons[1] were allotted one interviewee per 10,000 population unit, although very small cantons were guaranteed one regardless of size. An attempt was

1. Eleven cantons had to be omitted from the study because of extreme transportation problems.

made to apportion in such a manner that approximately one-third were purely local leaders, another third purely national leaders, and an intermediate third that—for lack of a better term—were called local-national liaison leaders or simply liaison leaders. However, since many respondents could not be accurately typed prior to interview, the final sample is heavily weighted in favor of local leaders. Criteria involved in typing the respondents involved an assessment of the individual's geographical base of partisan activity. Local leaders are those whose only area of party interest centers around the village, district, or canton.[2] They are seldom known outside the locality and take almost no part in the national party's affairs. At the other extreme, national leaders permanently reside in or near the capital, maintain no following in any particular locality (although they might maintain a broad following across the nation as a whole), and are intimately connected with the affairs of the nation and the affairs of the party at the national level. Members of this type do not usually participate in politics at the cantonal level and only come into contact with local leaders during organization drives or other partisan business. Liaison leaders are associated with, and usually reside in, a particular locality where they maintain political support, but they also spend much of their time in the capital. Liaison leaders usually have been legislators, ranking bureaucrats, or members of the National Directory and are known on close personal terms by national leaders. Although their influence is not as great in other parts of the nation as in their locality, liaison leaders often possess national reputations. The differences between each of the classifications were great enough that almost all could be arbitrarily typed without great doubt.

Within the cantons leaders were selected by a method that combined randomness with controls to include possible informal counterelites. Since one of the major hypotheses of chapter 5 concerns the existence of theoretical groups of PLN leaders opposed to the recognized formal ones, a completely random sample (based on final digits of membership certificates, for example) had to be ruled out. Instead, the opinions of local persons were matched against formal lists prepared at the

2. A few national leaders of the Juventud Liberacionista youth movement and the women's auxiliary whose range of activity did not cross over into the general party were also classified as local leaders.

National Liberation Party's headquarters in San José. Upon entering new cantons, the author asked a number of random persons whom they considered the most important PLN leaders in their community. In nearly all cases the opinions agreed with the formal list.

Sample Questionnaire

Position in Party _____

1. When did you join the Party?

2. Do you remember the exact reasons why you joined the Party?

3. How long ago did you begin to work actively in the electoral programs or organization of the Party?

4. How long have you occupied your present position in the Party?

5. Before beginning activities in the affairs of the Party, would you say Costa Rican politics: (1) interested you a great deal, (2) interested you moderately, or (3) did not interest you very much.

6. Did you take an active part in the 1948 Revolution?

6a. What was your function in the Army of National Liberation?

7. What other positions have you held in the Party?

8. Precisely, what is it you did (you are doing) to win the elections of 1966?

9. (If the interviewee is active only at the cantonal or local level.) In relation to your work in the Party, how often have you had contact with the most important provincial leaders?
   (1) Frequently, at least four times per year
   (2) Frequently during political campaigns, but almost never on other occasions
   (3) On rare occasions only
   (4) Almost never

10.   (If the interviewee is active at the local or provincial level.) Repeat the question changing the object to the national level.

11.   (Referring to number 9 and/or 10.) What type of things do you discuss with your superiors in the Party?

12.   How many PLN deputies in the 1962–66 Legislative Assembly are well known by you?

13.   Have you been a deputy in the Legislative Assembly?

14.   Do you believe a few strong leaders could make the country better than all the laws and studies that are made?

15.   Who in your opinion are the most influential PLN leaders in the country?

16.   (Only for local leaders.) Does the Party sponsor functions such as meetings, rallies, dances, picnics, et cetera in years in which there is no political campaign? What are those activities?

17.   Some persons believe that only a few leaders of the Party, or only a few closed groups, make the majority of decisions in the Party and also decide who will be its leaders in the future. Do you believe this is so? Why?

17a. If you believe this is so, do you consider yourself a member of such a group?

17b. (Only for local leaders.) Do such small groups affect the decisions of the Party in your locality? How?

17c. Are there similar small groups in your locality that make the majority of decisions?

18.   Almost all large political parties in the world have divisions and internal groups that rival each other at conventions, conferences, et cetera. Do you believe that the PLN has this type of divisions?

18a. Who are the leaders of each group in the Party?

18b. Over what type of issues do Party divisions become most heated?

18c. Would you say that the principal controversies between those groups are purely ideological or are based on the merits of certain leaders over others?

19.   (Only for local leaders.) Which of the various party wings you have just described is more popular among your friends and neighbors here in _____?

19a. Why is that group the most popular?

19b. Are there many liberacionistas here in _____ that sympathize with the group or leader that is not the most popular?

20.   Why do you believe the Party won the elections of 1953 and 1962?

21.   Why do you believe the Party lost the elections of 1958 (and 1966)?

22.   What do you suggest in order to insure the Party future victories?

23.   Many persons say that young people should be more strictly disciplined by their parents. Do you agree?

24.   Which of the persons on this list (show separate list) do you consider (1) very influential, (2) influential, or (3) a little influential in determining who people in general vote for?

   (a) Intimate friends
   (b) Relatives
   (c) Priests
   (d) Labor leaders
   (e) Bosses
   (f) Political leaders
   (g) Others (specify)

25. Do you really believe there are strong differences between the PLN and other political groups?

25a. What are those differences?

26. Why do you believe the PLN has grown so large since 1948?

27. Do you believe it is possible that the popular force of the PLN will diminish in future generations relative to other political groups?

28. From the standpoint of Costa Rican public opinion, in which aspect is the Party the most vulnerable?

29. Today there is opportunity for everyone and those that don't get ahead don't have ambition. Do you agree or not?

30. Many persons believe too much personalism exists in Latin American politics. Do you believe this is so?

30a. Do you believe this is true of Costa Rica?

30b. Was this true (or truer) of Costa Rica in the last generation?

31. What sort of candidates would you like to see nominated in 1970?

31a. Would you mind telling me the name of the presidential candidate you would prefer in 1970?

31b. Would you approve a change in the Constitution that would permit the consecutive re-election of the same person?

32. Many people say that an insult to personal honor or to honor of the family should not be forgotten. Do you agree?

Personal Data

   1. Age

   2. Sex

   3. Marital status

   4. Number of children

   5. To what religion do you belong?

   6. How many times do you go to church per month?

   7. Do you consider yourself:
       (a) Very religious
       (b) Moderately religious
       (c) Not very religious
       (d) Not religious at all

   8. Besides your activity in politics, what sort of work do you do?

9.   What was your occupation before joining the Party?

10.   What school did you attend?

10a. Did you graduate from the last school attended?

11.   What was the occupation of your father when you were a child?

12.   How long has your family been in Costa Rica?

13.   How long has your family lived in the locality where you now live?

Coding Procedures and Marginal Subtotals

1. Party Position: Leaders not currently active were typed according to the last position they held.
    - 7 (1) Member of National Directory
    - 7 (2) National leaders of Juventud Liberacionista
    - 2 (3) National leaders of Women's Auxiliary
    - 11 (4) Other national leaders
    - 32 (5) Members of provincial or cantonal executive committees
    - 4 (6) Former members of provincial or cantonal executive committees
    - 2 (7) Cantonal leaders of Juventud Liberacionista
    - 4 (8) Cantonal leaders of Women's Auxiliary
    - 14 (9) Other provincial or cantonal leaders
    - 20 (0) Leaders of district or neighborhood committees

2. Decisions concerning one of the three ranks of leaders, national, liaison, local, were made arbitrarily by the interviewer at the time of interview according to the criteria described above. Although an equal third was desired in each category, accurate typing prior to the interview proved difficult so the sample is heavily weighted in favor of local leaders.
    - 19 (1) National leaders
    - 29 (2) Liaison leaders
    - 55 (3) Local leaders

3. Period of Recruitment.
    - 9 (1) 1940 to 1945
    - 7 (2) 1946 to 1950
    - 52 (3) 1951 to 1955
    - 23 (4) 1956 to 1960
    - 12 (5) 1961 to 1966

4. Reason for joining party.
    - 27 (1) Ideological reasons
    - 9 (2) Power and influence reasons
    - 14 (3) Family and friends
    - 35 (4) Followers of don Pepe and 1948 Revolution
    - 1 (5) All four
    - 1 (6) 1 and 2
    - 5 (7) 1 and 3
    - 7 (8) 1 and 4
    - 3 (9) Other

5. Date of first active participation in PLN affairs.
    - 6 (1) 1940 to 1945
    - 4 (2) 1946 to 1950
    - 47 (3) 1951 to 1955
    - 24 (4) 1956 to 1960
    - 22 (5) 1961 to 1966

6. Tenure of present position.
   - 11 (1) Less than one year
   - 32 (2) 1 to 2 years
   - 31 (3) 3 to 4 years
   - 7 (4) 5 to 6 years
   - 5 (5) 7 to 8 years
   - 3 (6) 9 to 10 years
   - 1 (7) 11 to 12 years
   - 11 (8) More than 12 years
   - 3 (9) Not currently active

7. Interest in politics before joining PLN.
   - 64 (1) Very interested
   - 26 (2) Interested
   - 13 (3) Not interested

8. Did respondent take part in 1948 War?
   - 32 (1) Yes
   - 66 (2) No
   - 1 (3) Yes, but fought on the other side

9. Function in 1948 War?
   - 15 (1) Enlisted man on front
   - 5 (2) Officer on front
   - 5 (3) Procurer of supplies and weapons
   - 7 (4) Communications
   - 0 (5) Fund raiser
   - 1 (6) Other

10. Frequency of contact with provincial leaders. (Although the question was intended for local leaders only, practically everyone with a local base of activity was questioned; therefore, the totals are considerably more than fifty-five.)
    - 39 (1) Often
    - 28 (2) Frequently during campaign, but seldom in nonelection years
    - 13 (3) On rare occasions – at party conventions, gatherings, et cetera
    - 2 (4) Almost never
    - 18 (5) National leaders, not questioned

11. Frequency of contact with national leaders.
    - 24 (1) Often
    - 17 (2) Frequently during campaign, but seldom in nonelection years
    - 23 (3) On rare occasions – at party conventions, gatherings, et cetera
    - 20 (4) Almost never
    - 18 (5) National leaders, not questioned

12. What local leaders discuss with superiors. Since responses were varied and multiple, the following major groupings were coded horizontally on the data cards.
    - 20 (1) Party ideology and program
    - 14 (2) Current politics and governmental policy
    - 18 (3) General party organization and strength
    - 25 (4) Campaign techniques
    - 18 (5) The condition of the party in respondent's local community
    - 18 (6) Respondent's responsibilities in the Party
    - 12 (7) Questions regarding problems of local people

13. How many deputies of the 1962–66 Legislative Assembly are well known by the respondent?
    4 (1) None
    28 (2) 1 to 5
    26 (3) 6 to 10
    11 (4) 11 to 15
    6 (5) 16 to 20
    2 (6) 21 to 24
    4 (7) 25 to 28
    20 (8) All 29

14. Was respondent ever a deputy?
    20 (1) Yes
    81 (2) No

15. Belief that a few strong leaders can better national situation more than laws and studies.
    70 (1) Yes
    33 (2) No

16. Most influential leaders in the Party. (Coded horizontally on data cards.)
    100 (1)   José Figueres
    85 (2)   Daniel Oduber
    55 (3)   Francisco Orlich
    39 (4)   Alfonso Carro
    28 (5)   Rodolfo Solano Orfila
    44 (6)   Carlos Luis Jimenez Maffio
    41 (7)   Fernando Volio
    50 (8)   Rodrigo Carazo
    19 (9)   Alberto Cañas
    42 (10) Gonzalo Facio
    23 (11) Rafael Cordero
    13 (12) Hernan Garrón
    44 (13) Luis Alberto Monge
    9 (14) Benjamín Nuñez
    14 (15) Armando Arauz
    27 (16) José Luis Molina
    9 (17) Carlos Espinach

17. Does the PLN conduct activities in local areas during nonelection years?
    21 (1) Yes
    56 (2) No

18. Is PLN run by a small closed group?
    20 (1) Yes
    75 (2) No

19. Is the respondent a member of that small closed group?
    9 (1) Yes
    20 (2) No

20. (For local leaders only.) Does small closed group affect respondent's locality?
    9 (1) Yes
    16 (2) No

21. (For local leaders only.) Do small closed groups exist in respondent's locality?
    15 (1) Yes
    23 (2) No

22. Does PLN have internal factions?
    61 (1) Yes
    40 (2) No

23. Leaders of faction.
    21 (1) Progressive Oduber group versus Conservative Orlich group with
          Figueres ameliorating between them
    2 (2) Figueres included in Oduber faction
    2 (3) Figueres included in Orlich faction
    10 (4) Figueres not included
    0 (5) Some other form of Progressive-Conservative division
    4 (6) Jorge Rossi versus rest of Party in past
    0 (7) Young versus older party leaders
    4 (8) Other types of divisions

24. Nature of factional controversy. (Coded horizontally.)
    5 (1) Involving questions of economic development
    16 (2) Involving questions of social welfare and social justice
    13 (3) Involving questions of state regulation of business
    8 (4) Involving elections of party officers
    15 (5) Involving control of party machinery
    2 (6) Attitude toward communism
    4 (7) Other ideological-oriented responses
    0 (8) Other power-oriented responses

25. Are factions based on ideology or personal merit of groups of leaders?
    20 (1) Ideological
    12 (2) Personal merit
    13 (3) Both

26. Which faction is most popular in local community?
    19 (1) Progressive
    3 (2) Conservative
    1 (3) Center

27. Why is the faction more popular?
    19 (1) Ideological responses
    2 (2) Nonideological responses

28. Do many local persons favor the other faction?
    20 (1) Yes
    6 (2) No
    1 (3) People aren't aware of split

29. Why did PLN win the election of 1953? (Coded horizontally.)
    54 (1) Party's program and ideology (including popularity of Revolution of
          1948)
    58 (2) Popularity of candidate (including popularity of Revolution of 1948)
    7 (3) Most highly organized
    2 (4) Hatred of Calderón Guardia
    2 (5) Hatred of communism
    3 (6) Bad Ulate government
    4 (7) Other reasons

30. Why did PLN win the election of 1962? (Coded horizontally.)
    50 (1) Party's program and ideology (including popularity of 1948 Revolu-
          tion)
    18 (2) Popularity of candidate
    19 (3) Most highly organized

22 (4) Split in opposition
29 (5) Bad Echandi government
 7 (6) Other reasons

31. Why did PLN lose the election of 1958? (Coded horizontally.)
   3 (1) Party's program and ideology
   4 (2) Unpopularity of candidate
   4 (3) Other parties more highly organized
   5 (4) Unfortunate setbacks during Figueres government
   4 (5) Bad Figueres government
 78 (6) Faction of Jorge Rossi bolted party or party split
   7 (7) Other reasons

32. Why did PLN lose election of 1966? (Coded horizontally.)
   1 (1) Party program and ideology
   6 (2) Unpopularity of candidate
   5 (3) Other parties more highly organized
 21 (4) Apathy and disunity in PLN
   7 (5) Conservatives didn't work hard
   7 (6) Bad Orlich government
   7 (7) Charge of communism
 13 (8) Overconfidence
 16 (9) Fraud

33. What does respondent suggest to insure future victories?
 24 (1) Ideological suggestions
 11 (2) Give good government
 44 (3) Strengthen party machinery, throw out dead wood, et cetera
   5 (4) 1 and 2
   3 (5) 1 and 3
   0 (6) 2 and 3
   4 (7) Others

34. Should youth be disciplined more strictly?
 64 (1) Yes
 38 (2) No

35. Persons influential in determining voter decisions. (Coded horizontally.)

Close friends
75 (1) Very influential
19 (2) Moderately influential
 7 (3) Slightly influential

Relatives
78 (1) Very influential
14 (2) Moderately influential
 9 (3) Slightly influential

Priests
22 (1) Very influential
22 (2) Moderately influential
57 (3) Slightly influential

Labor leaders
 6 (1) Very influential
15 (2) Moderately influential
80 (3) Slightly influential

Bosses
18 (1) Very influential
37 (2) Moderately influential
46 (3) Slightly influential

Political leaders
78 (1) Very influential
19 (2) Moderately influential
 3 (3) Slightly influential

36. Are there really differences between PLN and other political groups?
94 (1) Yes
 9 (2) No

37. What are those differences?
60 (1) Ideological answers
11 (2) Nonideological answers
18 (3) Both

38. Why has the Party grown since 1948?
70 (1) Ideological
18 (2) Nonideological
 3 (3) Both

39. Belief that PLN will weaken in future.
36 (1) Yes
65 (2) No

40. Vulnerability of Party.
54 (1) Charge of communism
11 (2) Apathy
 0 (3) Dissension within the Party
 1 (4) Organizational reasons
 8 (5) Ideological reasons
 7 (6) Graft and corruption
 1 (7) Poor candidates
 4 (8) Other responses
 9 (9) Not vulnerable

41. Is there opportunity for all?
57 (1) Yes
46 (2) No

42. Is there too much personalism in Latin American politics?
87 (1) Yes
14 (2) No

43. Is there too much personalism in Costa Rican politics?
44 (1) Yes
57 (2) No

44. Was there more personalism in Costa Rican politics in the last generation?
93 (1) Yes
 5 (2) No

45. Type of presidential candidate respondent prefers in 1970.
43 (1) Ideological response
25 (2) Nonideological response

46. Approve consecutive re-election of same person.
48 (1) Yes
50 (2) No

47. Insult to honor should not be forgotten.
    25 (1) Yes
    78 (2) No

48. Age
     7 (1) Less than 25
    24 (2) 25 to 35
    29 (3) 36 to 45
    34 (4) 46 to 55
     8 (5) 56 to 65
     1 (6) Over 66

49. Sex
    91 (1) Male
    12 (2) Female

50. Marital Status
    82 (1) Married
    16 (2) Not married
     5 (3) Divorced

51. Number of children
     6 (1) One
     9 (2) Two
    13 (3) Three
    22 (4) Four
     7 (5) Five
    11 (6) Six
     5 (7) Seven
     2 (8) Eight
     6 (9) More than eight
    22 (0) None

52. Religion.
    93 (1) Catholic
     6 (2) Protestant
     2 (3) Jewish
     2 (4) No religion

53. Church attendance per month.
    35 (1) Never
    21 (2) Once (or seldom)
     6 (3) Twice
     4 (4) Three
    26 (5) Four
     9 (6) More than four

54. Regarding religion, respondent considers himself:
    29 (1) Very religious
    39 (2) Moderately religious
    26 (3) Not too religious
     9 (4) Not religious at all

55. Current occupation.
     5 (1) University professor
    17 (2) Lawyer
     5 (3) Physician
     7 (4) Schoolteacher
    10 (5) Other professional

7 (6)   Businessman
5 (7)   Rancher or landowner
4 (8)   Merchant
9 (9)   White-collar worker
7 (10) Public employee
2 (11) Urban-blue-collar worker
0 (12) Small farmer
0 (13) Farm worker
8 (14) Student
5 (15) Service
4 (16) Artisan
2 (17) Other
6 (18) Housewife

56. Occupation at time of entering PLN.
1 (1)   University professor
9 (2)   Lawyer
3 (3)   Physician
4 (4)   Schoolteacher
5 (5)   Other profession
3 (6)   Businessman
6 (7)   Rancher or landowner
3 (8)   Merchant
15 (9)   White-collar worker
1 (10)   Public employee
2 (11)   Urban-blue-collar worker
0 (12)   Small farmer
1 (13)   Farm worker
36 (14) Student
5 (15)   Service
3 (16)   Artisan
2 (17)   Other
4 (18)   Housewife

57. Education.
12 (1) Primary
19 (2) Secondary
48 (3) University
6 (4) Secondary abroad
9 (5) University abroad
3 (6) Trade or special school
6 (7) Normal school

58. Graduate from highest school attended?
75 (1) Yes
20 (2) No
8 (3) Not yet

59. Occupation of father.
0 (1)   University professor
5 (2)   Lawyer
8 (3)   Physician
2 (4)   Schoolteacher
12 (5)   Other profession
4 (6)   Businessman
9 (7)   Rancher or landowner

15 (8) Merchant
 7 (9) White-collar worker
 7 (10) Public employee
 7 (11) Urban-blue-collar worker
 8 (12) Small farmer
 8 (13) Farm worker
 0 (14) Student
 5 (15) Service
 2 (16) Artisan
 1 (17) Other

60. Length respondent's family has lived in Costa Rica.
     0 (1) Five years or less
     0 (2) 6 to 10 years
     1 (3) 11 to 20 years
     2 (4) 21 to 30 years
     2 (5) One generation
     8 (6) Two generations
    90 (7) More than two generations

61. Length respondent's family has lived in locality.
    13 (1) Five years or less
    13 (2) 6 to 10 years
    11 (3) 11 to 20 years
     4 (4) 21 to 30 years
     9 (5) One generation
     6 (6) Two generations
    46 (7) More than two generations

Bibliography

Public Documents

Costa Rica

Dirección General de Estadística y Censos. *1864 Censo de Población.* San José: Imprenta Nacional, reprinted 1964.

Figueres Ferrer, José, President of the Republic. *Cartas a un ciudadano.* San José: Imprenta Nacional, 1956.

———. *Doctrina social y jornales crecientes.* San José: Imprenta Nacional, 1949.

———. *Inaugural Address,* November 8, 1953. Official English Translation.

———. *Mensaje del Señor Presidente de la Junta Fundadora de la Segunda República.* San José: Imprenta Nacional, 1949.

———. *The Problems of Peace and the Problems of War.* San José: Imprenta Nacional, 1955.

Ministry of Foreign Affairs. *The Women's Vote in Costa Rica: How They Use Their Franchise.* San José: Imprenta Nacional, 1955.

United States

U.S. Senate, Committee on the Judiciary. "Communist Threat to the United States through the Caribbean," *Hearings Before the Subcommittee to Investigate the Administration of the Internal Security Act and Other Internal Security Laws of the Committee on the Judiciary.* Part 13, 87th Cong., March–July, 1961.

Books and Monographs

Alexander, Robert J. *Communism in Latin America.* New Brunswick, N.J.: Rutgers University Press, 1957.

Almond, Gabriel A., and Coleman, James S., eds. *The Politics of the Developing Areas.* Princeton, N.J.: Princeton University Press, 1960.

171

Biesanz, John, and Biesanz, Mavis. *Costa Rican Life.* New York: Columbia University Press, 1944.

Busey, James L. *Notes on Costa Rican Democracy.* Boulder: University of Colorado Press, 1962.

Cañas, Alberto F. *Los 8 años.* San José: Editorial Liberación Nacional, 1955.

Castro Esquivel, Arturo. *José Figueres Ferrer: El hombre y su obra.* San José: Imprenta Tormo, 1955.

Centro para el Estudio de Problemas Nacionales. *Ideario costarricense.* San José: Editorial Surco, 1943.

Chacón Trejos, Gonzalo. *Tradiciones Costarricenses.* San José: Editorial Letras Nacionales, 1956.

Chambers, William Nisbet. *Political Parties in a New Nation: The American Experience, 1776–1809.* New York: Oxford University Press, 1963.

Dauer, Manning J. *The Adams Federalists.* Baltimore, Md.: Johns Hopkins University Press, 1953.

Duverger, Maurice. *Political Parties: Their Organization and Activity in the Modern State.* New York: John Wiley and Sons, 1954.

Eldersveld, Samuel J. *Political Parties: A Behavioral Analysis.* Chicago: Rand McNally and Co., 1964.

Facio, Rodrigo. *Estudio sobre la economía costarricense.* San José: Editorial Surco, 1942.

Fernandez Guardia, Ricardo. *Cuentos Ticos (Short Stories of Costa Rica).* Translated by Case Gary. Cleveland: Burrow Bros., 1908.

Figueres, José. *Palabras Gastadas.* Mexico City, 1943; reprinted San José, 1955.

Goldrich, Daniel. *Sons of the Establishment: Elite Youth in Panama and Costa Rica.* Chicago: Rand McNally and Co., 1966.

La Guerra de la Liberación 1948. San José: Imprenta Atenea, 1949.

Guttman, L. "The Basis for Scalogram Analysis." In *Measurement and Prediction: Studies in Social Psychology in World War II,* edited by Samuel Stouffer, et al. Princeton, N.J.: Princeton University Press, 1950.

Kantor, Harry. *The Costa Rican Election of 1953: A Case Study.* Gainesville: University of Florida Press, 1958.

LaPalombara, Joseph, and Weiner, Myron. *Political Parties and Political Development.* Princeton, N.J.: Princeton University Press, 1966.

Lascaris C., Constantino. *Desarrollo de las ideas filosóficas en Costa Rica.* San José: Editorial Costa Rica, 1964.

Lasswell, Harold D. *Power and Personality.* New York: Norton Press, 1948.

———. *Psychopathology and Politics.* Chicago: University of Chicago Press, 1930.

Leiserson, Avery. *Parties and Politics.* New York: Alfred A. Knopf, 1958.

McDonald, Neil A. *The Study of Political Parties.* New York: Random House, 1955.

Martén, Alberto. *El Comunismo Vencido.* San José: Imprenta Borrase, 1962.

Monge A., Carlos. *Historia de Costa Rica.* 5th ed. San José: Editorial Fondo de Cultura de Costa Rica, 1953.

Morton, Ward M. *Castro as Charismatic Leader.* Lawrence: University of Kansas Press, 1965.

Nacionalización bancaria en Costa Rica. San José: Imprenta la Española, 1951.

Navarro Bolandi, Hugo. *José Figueres en la evolución de Costa Rica.* Mexico City: Imprenta Quirós, 1953.

Neumann, Sigmund, ed. *Modern Political Parties.* Chicago: University of Chicago Press, 1956.

Nuñez, Fr. Benjamín. *ABC del sindicalismo.* San José: Imprenta Española, 1945.

Obregón Loria, Rafael. *Conflictos militares y políticos de Costa Rica*. San José: Imprenta la Nación, 1951.
Ostrogorski, M. *Democracy and the Organization of Political Parties*. New York: Macmillan and Co., 1902.
Quijano Quesada, Alberto. *Costa Rica ayer y hoy*. San José: Editorial Borrase, 1939.
Rodriguez Vega, Eugenio. *Apuntes para una sociología Costarricense*. San José: Editorial Universitario, 1953.
Stephenson, Paul G. *Costa Rican Election Factbook, February 6, 1966*. Washington: Institute for the Comparative Study of Political Systems, 1966.
Weber, Max. "Politik als Beruf." In *Gesammelte Politische Schriften*. Munich: Duncker and Humboldt, 1921.

Articles and Periodicals

"Acción del Centro: Algunos de nuestros conceptos políticos." *Diario de Costa Rica*, 28 July 1943.
"Acción del Centro: Cambios democráticos en los sistemas electorales; voto femenino." *Diario de Costa Rica*, 2 June 1943.
"Acción del Centro: Por la cooperativización de la propriedad enemiga." *Diario de Costa Rica*, 7 July 1943.
"Acción del Centro: Reformar electorales; prohibición de actividades políticas a los empleados públicos." *Diario de Costa Rica*, 14 May 1943.
Acción Demócrata. 1943–1951. Changed in 1947 to *El Social Demócrata*.
"Acción Demócrata y el capitalismo nacional." *Acción Demócrata*, 18 March 1944, p. 2.
"Ante el pacto Republicano Nacional-Vanguardia Popular." *Surco*, no. 40, October 1943, pp. 1–6.
"Audaz mentira anda divulgando D. Mario Echandi." *El Social Demócrata*, 31 July 1948, p. 1.
Brenes, Roberto. "Cooperativos de consumo en haciendas." *Surco*, no. 53, June 1945, pp. 19–21.
Busey, James L. "The Presidents of Costa Rica." *The Americas*, 18, no. 1, July 1961, p. 61.
Cañas, Alberto F. "El país está maduro para la formación de un partido ideológico democrático." *Surco*, no. 42, December 1943, p. 1.
———. "Propaganda politiquero y propaganda política." *Surco*, no. 43, January 1944, p. 1.
Castillo, Carlos Manuel. "El Partido ideológico es necesidad en Costa Rica." *Acción Demócrata*, 27 May 1944, p. 3, and 4 June 1944, p. 4.
"El Centro: Un generación, un programa, un partido." *Diario de Costa Rica*, 15 March 1944, p. 3.
"El 'Centro' llama a la compactación." *Diario de Costa Rica*, 18 February 1944, p. 1.
"El Centro piensa: Campaña de cultura cívica democrática." *La Hora*, 20 July 1943.
"La ciudadanía sabe bien que el Centro no tiene ningún nexo con el gobierno ni con el comunismo." *Diario de Costa Rica*, 20 August 1943, p. 1.
"Como funciona Acción Demócrata." *Acción Demócrata*, 4 March 1944, p. 1.
"Complementos necesarios de las garantías sociales." *Diario de Costa Rica*, 28 April 1943.
"De la declaración de principios y de los estatutos del Centro." *Surco*, no. 13, June 1941, p. 16.

"Desarrollo del programa: Objectivo inmediato de la política económica social." *Acción Demócrata,* 19 January 1946.

Diario de Costa Rica. 1940–1950.

"Dice el Centro: Mientras nuestra producción sea insuficiente, poco se avanzará con imponer precios oficiales a las cosas." *La Hora,* 30 March 1943.

"Emplasamos al Partido Vanguardia Popular en Defensa de Nuestra Democracia Política." *Diario de Costa Rica,* 6 August 1943, p. 1.

"Es urgente un frente unido de la oposición." *Acción Demócrata,* 1 September 1945, p. 2.

Facio, Rodrigo. "Ensayos cooperativos en Costa Rica." *Surco,* no. 31, January 1943, pp. 30–33.

Facio Segreda, Gonzalo. "Al margen del debate eléctrico." *Surco,* no. 12, May 1941, pp. 6–8.

————. "Necesidad de los partidos políticos doctrinales en la democracia." *Surco,* no. 13, June 1941, p. 3.

————. "Ni la Constitución ni los Fines, ni la trayectoria de los tres partidos en lucha podían nunca satifacer el Anhelo que nos Une." *Diario de Costa Rica,* 15 July 1943, p. 1.

Fernandez, Gerardo. "En defensa de nuestra democracia." *Surco,* no. 38, August 1943, p. 3.

Figueres Ferrer, José. "La América de Hoy." *Combate,* 2, July–August 1959, pp. 8–13.

————. "Carta a un Ciudadano." *Boletín del Secretariado Latino-americano de la Internacional Socialista,* 2, no. 7, March–April 1958, pp. 146–47.

————. "Democracia." *Acción Demócrata,* 17 June 1944, p. 3.

————. "Establización del café." *Combate,* 3, no. 17, July–August 1960, pp. 41–43.

————. "Estados Unidos y América Latina." *Boletín del Secretariado Latino-americano de la Internacional Socialista,* 2, no. 10, July 1958, pp. 203–4.

————. "My Political Testament." *Socialist International Information,* 15, no. 6, September 1965, pp. 63–65.

————. "La Revolución en Latinoamérica." *Política y Espíritu,* 3, 15 August 1959, pp. 9–12.

"La formación de un 'Frente Unido Oposicionista' ha sido planteada por el Partido Social Demócrata." *Acción Demócrata,* 21 September, 1946, p. 1.

Fournier, Fernando. "Los Estados Unidos de F. D. Roosevelt." *Surco,* no. 15, August 1941, pp. 10–11.

Gonzalez Gutierrez, Hernán. "El sistema personalista político." *Surco,* no. 36, June 1943, pp. 15–17.

"Hacía la formación del Partido Político Doctrinario: El Centro es un organización permanente." *Diario de Costa Rica,* 23 February 1944, p. 1.

"Haga conocer a todas nuestros 12 postulados." *Surco,* no. 53, June 1945, pp. 18–19.

Haya de la Torre, Victor Raul. "Frente único, y no lucha clasista." *Acción Demócrata,* 12 May 1945, p. 3.

"Ideas y figuras del socialismo democrático." *El Social Demócrata,* 27 May 1950.

"Información sobre las secciones del Centro." *Surco,* no. 35, May 1943, p. 5.

Juventud Liberacionista. *Surco Nuevo,* 1963–1966.

Kantor, Harry. "La colaboración entre los partidos." *Panoramas,* no. 12, November–December 1964, pp. 67–76.

Lane, Robert E. "Political Personality and Electoral Choice." *American Political Science Review,* 49, March 1955, pp. 173–90.

Lombardo Toledano, Vicente. "Organizaciones de planificación cooperativas de consumo por tierras de América: Vicente Lombardo Toledano habla para *Surco*." *Surco,* no. 31, January 1943, pp. 5–7.

Lowland, Paul. "Costa Rica: Una Situación Difícil." *Boletín del Secretariado*

Latinoamericano de la Internacional Socialista, 2, no. 11, August–September 1958, pp. 225–26.

McGovern, Joseph J. "The Costa Rican Labor Movement: A Study in Political Unionism." *Public and International Affairs*, 4, no. 1, Spring 1966, pp. 88–116.

Madrigal N., Rodrigo. "Haya de la Torre y el Aprismo." *Surco*, no. 50, October 1944, p. 11.

Martz, John D. "Costa Rican Electoral Trends, 1953–1966." *The Western Political Quarterly*, 20, no. 4, December 1967, pp. 888–909.

"El máximo problema de Costa Rica es el de que toda su riqueza aún no ha sido explotada." *Diario de Costa Rica*, 30 November 1943, p. 9.

"Mensaje de la Conferencia Internacional Socialista." *El Social Demócrata*, 13 May 1950.

Monge, Carlos. "El Liberalismo en Costa Rica." *Surco*, no. 43, January 1944, pp. 8–9.

————. "Vieja y nueva política." *Surco*, no. 44, February 1944, p. 8.

Monge, Luis Alberto. "No hay Revolución sin Libertad." *Combate*, no. 18 (1961), p. 31.

Morúa, Luis F. "Hacía la formación de un partido de frente único." *Surco*, no. 37, July 1943, pp. 20–22.

"Muy avanzadas los negociones para la fusión de los movimientos de Acción Demócrata y el Centro para el Estudio de Problemas Nacionales." *Acción Demócrata*, 7 April 1944, p. 1.

"Muy avanzados los trabajos para la fusión con el Centro." *Acción Demócrata*, 15 July 1944, p. 1.

La Nación. 1957–1966.

The New York Times. 1948–1966.

Orlich, Francisco J. "Hacía adonde vamos; Mensaje presidencial." *Combate*, 4, no. 22, May–June 1962, pp. 9–15.

"Otro triunfo del pueblo." *El Social Demócrata*, 11 August 1947, p. 1.

"El país está maduro para la formación de un partido ideológico democrático." *Surco*, no. 42, January 1943, pp. 1–3.

"El país está maduro para vivir en un régimen de Partido Ideológicos." *Diario de Costa Rica*, 3 March 1944, p. 1.

"El Partido Comunista de Costa Rica enjuiciado por sus hechos." *Surco*, no. 37, July 1943, p. 31.

"El Partido Doctrinario contra la política personalista." *Acción Demócrata*, 7 April 1945, p. 3.

"El Partido Social Demócrata le ofrece su cooperación al Presidente Avévalo de Guatemala." *Acción Demócrata*, 7 April 1945.

"El Partido Social Demócrata y la mujer costarricense." *Mundo Femenino*, 29 November 1948.

"Pensamos: El movimiento cooperativo, el Partido Comunista y el Centro." *Surco*, no. 28, October 1942, pp. 1–4.

"La Política Social." *Surco*, no. 47, May–June 1944, p. 51.

La Prensa Libre. 1949.

"Programa ideológico del Partido Social Demócrata presentado al Registro Electoral." *El Social Demócrata*, 2 October 1948.

La República. 1951–1966.

Robinson, W. S. "Ecological Correlations and the Behavior of Individuals." *American Sociological Review*, 15 (1950), pp. 351–57.

Rossi, Jorge. "Una visita a la Empresa San Cristóbal de José Figueres." *Acción Demócrata*, 7 April 1944, p. 1.

"Sensacional manifesto dirige al país 'Acción Demócrata.'" *Diario de Costa Rica*, 29 February 1944, p. 1.

"Socialismo y Cultura." 1944. Mimeographed.

Surco. 1940–1945.
"'Teoría y realidad del 'Bloque de la Victoria.'" *Surco*, no. 51, December 1944 and January 1945, pp. 1–4.
"Urge crear un gran frente único de reivindicación." *Acción Demócrata*, 16 June 1945.
Valverde, Emilio. "Origen y desarrollo de las cooperativas." *Surco*, no. 31, January 1943, p. 21.
Yochelson, John. "What Price Political Stability? The 1966 Presidential Campaign in Costa Rica." *Public and International Affairs*, 5, no. 1 (1967), pp. 279–307.
Zúñiga, Rafael Alberto. "Hacía una política económica definida." *Surco*, no. 25, July 1942, p. 8.
_____. "La importancia del sistema cooperativo en Costa Rica." *Surco*, no. 40, October 1943, pp. 12–17.
_____. "Prepárese la ciudadanía costarricense para vivir en el régimen de la opinión pública al traves de la voluntád política de los partidos ideológicos." *Surco*, no. 29, November 1942, p. 1.
_____. "Principios administrativos de las cooperativas." *Surco*, no. 31, January 1943, p. 21.

Party Pamphlets, Brochures, Reports, and Documents

Acción Demócrata. *Actas Oficiales*. 1943–1945. *Party Pamphlets, Brochures, Reports, and Documents*.
_____. "Declaración de Principios y Reglamento Interno." San José, 1943.
Centro para el Estudio de Problemas Nacionales. *Actas Oficiales*. 1940–1945.
_____. "El Centro para el Estudio de Problemas Nacionales y el trabajador costarricense." Archives of the Center for the Study of National Problems. San José. Unauthored commission report. Typewritten.
_____. "Programa del 'Centro para el Estudio de Problemas Nacionales.'" Archives of the Center for the Study of National Problems. San José. Unpublished manuscript, circa 1944.
_____. "Quienes somos." San José, circa 1941.
Figueres Ferrer, José. *Dos Revoluciones: La Revolución Cubana y la Alianza para el Progreso*. San José: Editorial Eloy Morúa Carrillo, 1962.
_____. "Liberación Nacional ante la Revolución Cubana." Speech given January 5, 1962 during the electoral campaign of don Francisco Orlich. Printed.
Gil Pacheco, Rufino. *La nacionalización bancaria*. San José: Editorial "Eloy Morúa," 1962.
"Informe anual de tesorería; Período 1° Marzo 1945 a 30 Abril 1946." Archives of the Social Democratic Party. San José. Mimeographed.
"Informe de la comisión nombrada por la Asamblea Ejecutiva para el estudio de la posible coordinación de funciones de Acción Demócrata y el Centro de Estudio para los Problemas Nacionales [sic]." Archives of Acción Demócrata. San José. Typewritten.
Juventud Liberacionista de Costa Rica. *Un programa económico específico para Costa Rica*. Circa 1962. Mimeographed.
Letter from Rafael Ángel Chavarría, President of the Executive Assembly of Acción Demócrata, to the National Secretary of the Center for the Study of National Problems. September 11, 1944. Archives of Acción Demócrata. San José.
Letter from Carlos José Gutierrez, Secretary General of the Social Democratic

Party, to members of the San José provincial committee. July 14, 1948. Archives of the Social Democratic Party. San José.

Letter from Eloy Morúa, Secretary General of the Social Democratic Party, to Otilio Ulate. September 10, 1947. Archives of the Social Democratic Party. San José.

Letter from Otilio Ulate to the Social Democratic Executive Convention. October 17, 1948. Archives of the Social Democratic Party. San José.

Madrigal, Rodrigo. "El Centro ante el cooperativismo." Archives of the Center for the Study of National Problems. San José. Unpublished committee report, 1943.

Memorandum from Luis Alberto Monge to members of the National Executive Committee. September 3, 1963.

Minutes of the combined executive committees of the Center for the Study of National Problems and Democratic Action. 1944–1945.

Morúa, Luis F. "El A.P.R.A., modelo de los movimientos políticos-sociales en indoamérica." Archives of the Center for the Study of National Problems. San José. Report for the Center's Commission on Social and Economic Affairs.

Movimiento Liberación Nacional. Minutes of the Plenary Council, 1951–1954. Source withheld upon request.

Oduber, Daniel. "Discurso de la campaña electoral." San José: Editorial Eloy Morúa Carrillo, 1965.

_____. De Donde Venimos. San José: Editorial Eloy Morúa Carrillo, 1965.

_____. La educación, la mujer y la política. San José: Editorial Eloy Morúa Carrillo, 1965.

_____. "Mensaje a los trabajadores." San José: Editorial Eloy Morúa, 1965.

Orlich, Francisco. Plataforma Política para la administración Orlich, 1958–1962. San José, 1957.

Partido Independiente. El Partido Independiente defiende la Constitución y las leyes. San José: Librería e Imprenta las Americas, 1957.

_____. El Partido Independiente es Voz de Dignidad y de Moral. San José, 1957.

Partido Liberación Nacional. "Carta Fundamental." San José. Various printings, 1951–1966.

_____. Estatutos (May, 1965).

_____. Nuestro programa de Trabajo, 1966–1970. San José, 1966.

_____. Plataforma Política. 1958, 1962, and 1966. Printed or Mimeographed.

_____. Programa económica. San José: Editorial Eloy Morúa Carrillo, 1962–1966.

_____. "Programa de Educación." San José: Editorial Eloy Morúa Carrillo, circa 1964.

_____. El trabajador y el Partido Liberación Nacional. San José, 1965.

_____. Secretaría de Capacitación. Nuestra economía. San José, circa 1960.

Partido Social Demócrata. Actas Oficiales. 1945–1951.

_____. Résumen del Programa del Gobierno del Partido Social Demócrata. San José, circa 1948.

Rodriguez V., Eugenio. "Hacía una verdadera justicia social." Archives of the Center for the Study of National Problems. San José. Unpublished and undated committee report.

Dissertations, Theses, and Manuscripts

Figueres, José. "Wages." Unpublished manuscript in the library of José Figueres, 1966.

Stephenson, Paul G. "Costa Rican Government and Politics." Ph.D. dissertation, Emory University, 1965.

Wolff, John F. "José Figueres of Costa Rica: His Theory and Politics as a Model for Latin American Development and Security." Master's thesis, University of Florida, 1962.

Worthington, Wayne L. "The Costa Rican Public Security Forces: A Model Armed Force for Emerging Nations?" Master's thesis, University of Florida, 1966.

Cited Interviews

Figueres, José. San José, 29 March 1966.
Gutierrez, Carlos José. San José, 15 March 1966.
Nuñez, Fr. Benjamín. San José, 29 April 1966.
Vargas Vargas, Hernán. Liberia, Costa Rica, 14 April 1966.
Volio, Fernando. San José, 26 May 1966.

Index

ACOSTA, Oton: early CEPN activist, 24
AE scale. *See* Lane, Robert E.
Age: in relation to leadership structure of PLN, 56–57
Agricultural workers: in relation to electoral support base of PLN, 106–8
Alvarado, Fermín: activities within youth organization, 71
Álvarez, Rafael Angel: appointed auditor for Department of Prisons, 44
Americans for Democratic Action (United States): expression of support, 133
Aprista Movement. *See* Haya de la Torre, Victor Raul; Aprista Party of Peru
Aprista Party of Peru: as example of modern party, 4; PLN turns away from ideology, 128–29; example of Popular Party, 131, 149; as probable nonpersonalist party of future, 154; development outside governmental circles, 156. *See also* Haya de la Torre, Victor Raul
Arauz, Armando: early activist in PLN youth organization, 70; labor organizer, 144
Authentic Cortesista Party: joins antigovernment coalition, 39
Authoritarian-Equalitarian (AE) scale. *See* Lane, Robert E.
Authoritarianism: in relation to PLN leadership recruitment, 61 ff.; in

relation to intraparty communication, 84–85
Azofeifa, Felipe: organizer of student discussion groups, 17
Azofeifa, Isaac: early CEPN activist, 24; elected to Executive Council of PSD, 32

BEECHE, Ricardo: coordinated antigovernment convention, 39
Betancourt, Rómulo: as charismatic leader, 156. *See also* Democratic Action of Venezuela
Blanco, Raul: appointed Minister of Public Health, 44; President of Directory of National Liberation Movement, 51
Blue-collar workers: in relation to electoral support base of PLN, 108–9
Brenes Mesén, Roberto: object of Communist attack, 21; informal advisor of CEPN, 24
Busey, James L.: work on Costa Rican military, 12

CACIQUISMO: as an impediment to intraparty democracy, 77
Calderón Guardia, Rafael Angel: formed coalition with Communists, 20; signs pact with Ulate, 40; loses election, 40; supporters launch war from Nicaragua, 73–74; as exiled partisan leader, 93; presidential candidate, 95; as factor in PLN victory, 98; long-term effects of

179

Economic program: development, 124 ff.

Education: in relation to leadership structure of PLN, 56 ff.; in relation to electoral support base of PLN, 109–10

Elections: during traditional period, 9; hostilities in 1944, 20 ff.; overview of four elections, 93 ff.

Esquivel, Mario: elected treasurer of PLN, 52

FACIO, Gonzalo: early CEPN activist, 24; appointed Minister of Justice, 44; as leader of conservative wing, 87

Facio, Rodrigo: instructed courses in political economy, 19; undeclared intellectual leader of CEPN, 24; discusses merger, 30; elected to Executive Council of PSD, 32; heads Department of Propaganda of PSD, 36; congressional candidate, 38; concepts of property, 125–26

Fallas, Otto: labor organizer, 144

Fernandez, Gerardo: statement regarding personalist parties, 121–22

Fernandez, Julia, de Cortes. See Cortes, Julia Fernandez

Figueres Ferrer, José (Don Pepe): congressional nomination, 27; biographical data, 27 ff.; elected to Executive Council of PSD, 32; resigns from PSD, 37; coordinated antigovernment convention, 39; elected Chief of Action of United Opposition, 39; demands overthrow of government, 40; charges against him, 43 ff.; relations with Ulate worsen, 44–47; establishes PLN, 47 ff.; Chief of National Liberation Movement, 51; nominated presidential candidate, 52; involved in dispute with Carazo, 54; relationships with Liberationist Youth, 72–73; pivotal figure in PLN, 88; 1953 presidential candidate, 93 ff.; as factor in electoral victory, 97–98; charisma as factor in early PLN support base, 116–17; concepts of property, 125; relations with United States political groups, 133; detailed consideration of political and social thought, 134 ff.; support

for public education, 144–45; uses charisma to found party, 147; effects of charisma reviewed, 149; appeal to wide segments of population, 154; as charismatic leader, 156

Finance of PLN, 75–77

Founding Junta of the Second Republic: established, 41; accomplishments, 41 ff.

Fournier, Fernando: early CEPN activist, 24

Frei, Eduardo: charismatic leader of Christian Democrats in Chile, 156

Fundamental Charter of PLN, 49 ff.

GAMBOA, Emma: led march, 40

Gamez, Uladislao: appointed Minister of Public Education, 44

Garron, Francisco: leader of conservative wing, 87

Generation gap: cause for split in PLN, 53–54

Generation of '48: as leadership cadre of new party, 147. See also Center for the Study of National Problems; Democratic Action; Figueres, José; War of National Liberation

Goicoechea, Alfonso: early AD activist, 26; discusses merger, 30; involved in dispute with Fernando Valverde, 52

Goldrich, Daniel: work on political recruitment in Costa Rica, 117

Gomez, Alexis: activities within JL, 71

Gonzalez, Cecilia de Penrod. See Penrod, Cecilia Gonzalez

Guardia, General Tomás, 11

Guevara, Ernesto (Ché): hero to extreme elements of JL, 131

Gutierrez, Carlos José: early CEPN activist, 24

Guttman, Louis: work on Guttman Scales, 61 ff.

HAYA DE LA TORRE, Victor Raul: political thought as model to older PLN activists, 53, 119 ff.; influence of economic program, 124 ff.; review of influence on early PLN activities, 149; caudillo of Aprista Party, 154; as charismatic leader, 156. See also Aprista Party of Peru

Hernandez, Mario: discusses merger, 30

Mora Valverde, Manuel: signed agreement forming coalition, 20; involving support for Oduber, 96; support in plantation areas, 107–8. *See also* Popular Vanguard Party

Morton, Ward M.: work on charismatic personalities, 153 ff.

Morúa, Eloy: early activist in Democratic Action, 26; editor of partisan journal, 27; invites participation from CEPN, 30; appointed Chief of National Office of Information, 44; founder of PLN youth organization, 70; killed, 70

NATIONAL CONCILIATION PARTY OF EL SALVADOR: example of "government" party, 156

National Institute of Housing and Urbanism (INVU): establishment and functions, 142

National Liberation Movement: compared to National Liberation Party, 49 ff.; consideration of renewal after 1966 defeat, 53–54

National Republican Party: established, 155. *See also* Republican Party; Calderón Guardia, Rafael Angel

National Revolutionary Party of Bolivia: example of Popular Party, 132

National Unification Party (PUN₁): creation, 96–97

National Union Party (PUN): joins antigovernment coalition, 38; activity in national elections, 93 ff.; merger with PRN, 96–97; electoral support base compared to PLN, 113–15; future prospects of merger, 149; institutionalization, 153; future prospects, 155. *See also* Ulate, Otilio; Echandi, Mario

Neumann, Sigmund: work on party establishment, 5

Nomination process, 77–79

Nuñez, Benjamin: appointed Minister of Labor, 44; leader of PLN left wing, 54; work in Costa Rican labor movement, 143–44

OBREGÓN VALVERDE, Enrique: presidential candidate, 95

Occupation: in relation to leadership structure of PLN, 58 ff.

Oduber, Daniel: early CEPN activist, 24; relationships with Liberationist Youth, 71–72; leader of leftist wing, 87; presidential candidate, 96; accused of Communist sympathies, 96; as factor in PLN electoral defeat, 99; concepts of democratic socialism, 131–32; attitudes toward labor unions, 143; support from organized labor, 144; support for public education, 144

Orlich, Francisco: supports speech by Figueres, 29; elected to Executive Council of PSD, 32; congressional candidate, 38; represents PSD at antigovernment convention, 38; appointed Minister of Public Works, 44; establishes PLN, 48 ff.; elected President of PLN, 52; chairman of political committee of National Liberation Movement, 52; favors PLN women's organization, 73; leader of conservative wing, 87; presidential candidate, 94 ff.; as factor in PLN defeat, 98–99

PARLIAMENTARY FRACTION OF PLN, 74–75

Patio de Agua Group: program of leftist dissidents in PLN, 54; support from Liberationist Youth, 72; support for Oduber, 144

Penrod, Cecilia Gonzalez: activities in women's organization of PLN, 73

Peña, Antonio: elected to Executive Council of PSD, 32; congressional candidate, 38

Picado, Teodoro: presidential candidate, 20

Plan of Universal Capitalization: economic program of PLN, 141 ff.

Political parties: criteria for the study of, 6–7; theories of party establishment, 149 ff.

Popular Democratic Action Party (PADP): supported by Communists, 95. *See also* Obregón Valverde, Enrique

Popular Parties of Latin America: PLN turns away from ideology, 128–29; relations with PLN, 132 ff.

Popular Vanguard Party (PVP): charges of armed attacks, 40; outlawed, 41–42; untypical of Communists, 43; activities in 1953 election, 94;

LATIN AMERICAN MONOGRAPHS — SECOND SERIES